A WIDOW'S PRAYER

FINDING GOD'S GRACE
IN THE DAYS AHEAD

NELL E. NOONAN

UPPER
ROOM BOOKS®
NASHVILLE

Cover and interior design: Bruce Gore | Gore Studio, Inc.

Library of Congress Cataloging-in-Publication Data

Noonan, Nell E.
  A widow's prayer : finding God's grace in the days ahead / Nell E. Noonan.
      pages cm
  ISBN 978-0-8358-1506-2 (print)—ISBN 978-0-8358-1535-2 (mobi)—
  ISBN 978-0-8358-1507-9 (epub)
1. Widows—Prayers and devotions. I. Title.
  BV4908.N66 2015
  242'.6434—dc23
                        2015001128

Printed in the United States of America

With gratitude beyond words
I dedicate this book to
three beautiful, remarkable, resilient women:
My mother, Nell,
My daughter, Elizabeth,
My sister, Mary.

And to my generous spiritual mentor,
the Right Reverend Sam B. Hulsey

CONTENTS

HEALING AND HOPE

Mourning to Morning

FOREWORD

Thanks be, Nell Noonan has done it again! Her previous work has helped so many of us, and now she is not "wasting the pain" of her beloved Bob's death but sharing her experiences honestly, vulnerably, and lovingly. Her warmth and humor are gifts to those who are often lonely, confused, and sad. In this book, she writes especially for widows.

We reach for the goal of transformation—becoming healthier body, mind, and soul, seeking renewal by following the crucified and risen Lord on the eternal route of new beginnings, and becoming more servant-like. Nell, in this process herself, is able to help so many others.

Nell's personal scriptural motto could be Psalm 84:5: "Those who go through the desolate valley will find it a place of springs" (BCP). We have to travel, usually slowly, through the desolate valley. Nell reminds us that this journey takes time and must be done in our own way. But at the end, we will find a place of springs. Thanks be to God for her work.

—THE RIGHT REVEREND SAM B. HULSEY

ACKNOWLEDGMENTS

I wrote this book from my experience of my husband Bob's last weeks and the twenty-six months that followed. I am deeply grateful to those who aided me during that time of transition. I thank Christian Care Hospice, the staff and residents of Lakewood Village in Fort Worth, Texas, and the staffs and church families of Saint Barnabas United Methodist Church in Arlington, Texas, and the congregation at Duke Chapel in Durham, North Carolina.

My family and friends provided incredible, loving support. My mother, children, and grandchildren were major sources of strength, comfort, and joy. I am especially grateful to my daughter, Elizabeth, and her husband, Mike Schoenfeld, and my sister, Mary.

I thank these special friends: Emily and Mike Williams, Nancy and Dick Meyer, Frances Hennigan, Una Ronné, and Beverly Dowdy.

I owe an immense debt of gratitude to the Right Reverend Sam B. Hulsey for his spiritual direction, encouragement, and support through many years, as well as his hands-on involvement in my writing projects, including this one. He also connected me with the Reverend Stuart Hoke whose spiritual direction has been helpful and meaning-filled after my relocation to North Carolina.

Special thanks go to Anabel Stehli for her editorial critique and insightful suggestions. She challenged me to seek excellence in my written words while extending encouragement and affirmation during every step of this project.

Last but not least I thank Jeannie Crawford-Lee and her team at Upper Room Books for believing in this project and for bringing it to readers.

And to God be the glory. Amen.

INTRODUCTION

The steadfast love of the LORD never ceases,
his mercies never come to an end;
they are new every morning;
great is [God's] faithfulness.

LAMENTATIONS 3:22-23

During morning prayers on the first anniversary of my husband Bob's death, I experienced a quickening of my spirit telling me to write about my journey in grief, not only in my journals but also in a collection of devotions dedicated to other widows. I think of these women as my tribe, my sisters. There are millions of us, all mourning differently after an intense loss. My odyssey is unique. My writing is not meant to tell you what or how or when to do anything. The devotions are only meant to hold your hand and feel your pain so that hopefully you will be able to inch slowly, step-by-step, into being more whole, less broken—into a new peace-filled life.

My fond hope is to encourage you to engage in self-care by setting aside time each day to pray, read scripture, and abide in the Lord's presence. We are spiritual beings, and our spirituality needs nourishment and exercise in the same way that our bodies and minds do. Praying and writing are acts of deep vulnerability and intentional openness. If you are not in the practice of keeping a journal, you might want to consider doing so. Those of us who write and pray this way have discovered that when we write regularly and honestly, we encounter far more than we imagined. We encounter Holy Mystery, we encounter God, and we encounter the Love that will not let us go.

This journey in grief has been packed with brokenness and blessings. My spiritual director often asks me, "What is God teaching your heart today?" God is teaching my heart that God is more mysterious and elusive than ever, and yet the paradox is that God is more real and nearer than ever. Another primary lesson I am learning is gratitude. The loss will not fully go away. Yet as time passes, that void diminishes, and I focus on the gifts of love and friendship that never die. I think about my beloved Irishman now and remember the joy of life with him. I count blessings for what I had and what I have—not what I've lost. Love leaves memories that cannot be stolen.

Another lesson, forced upon me, has been patience with unsolved questions and unresolved issues. Waiting is uncomfortable for most of us, but forcing resolutions does not work. Healing takes time, and some questions are open-ended, not to be answered. Living in the moment and experiencing each day fully invites us out of darkness and self-preoccupation to a place of light, contentment, peace, and a desire to share our "bread" with others. How it happens is mind-boggling, but God surprises seekers all the time. "From [God's] fullness we have all received, grace upon grace" (John 1:16).

The devotions fall into four phases of my journey in grief: the first six months of deep grief, then several months when the grief began to soften. After the first year, I began pondering my identity: Who am I and what is my purpose in life? The fourth and final group of devotions expresses experiences of joy and acceptance of my changed life that features a stronger desire to serve. I would not reshape the crucible of grief that has made me a better person. The wilderness I encountered has deepened and expanded my compassion for myself and for others. Thanks be to God.

Satisfy us in the morning with your steadfast love,
so that we may rejoice and be glad all our days. . . .
Let the favor of the LORD our God be upon us,
and prosper for us the work of our hands.
PSALM 90:14, 17

SORROW, SIGHING, AND CONSOLATION

Then when you call upon me
and come and pray to me, I will hear you.

JEREMIAH 29:12

LAST WORDS

READ ROMANS 8:35, 37-39.

I am convinced that neither death nor life, . . .
will be able to separate us from the love of God
that is in Christ Jesus our Lord.

ROMANS 8:38-39, NIV

These are journal entries made during my husband's last days:

Tuesday, April 17—Feeling exhausted. Saw Bob's doctor yesterday, and Christian Care Hospice has now been set up here at home. Lord, I am depressed and so very weary.

Thursday, April 19—My Lord, it's happening so fast. A sitter is with him now so I can shop and run errands. Daughter Elizabeth comes Saturday and daughter-in-law Alice on Tuesday. Social worker, hospice chaplain, and our pastor came yesterday. Keep my Bob peaceful, dear Lord, and help him delight in his homecoming. I don't think he is going to stay with us but a few more days.

Monday, April 23—Bob loved talking and laughing with Elizabeth Saturday (so glad she got some time with the stepdad she adores). He was losing ability to communicate by last night . . . fell many times over the weekend. Sometimes I couldn't get him up and had to call the firemen to come put him back in his bed or his chair. He's so restless . . . body shutting down. The second time the firemen came last night, one of them said, "I've watched you, lady, more than a year now. This is killing you. It's time for him to go some place; you can't do it anymore." I knew he was right; I could no longer deal with the situation physically. I made arrangements and the medical transport folks came and moved Bob to a hospice room in the skilled nursing wing of our retirement facility. Grateful though I was for the help I needed, O Lord, it was gut-wrenching to watch him leave our home for the last time.

Tuesday, April 24—Many visitors—beautiful friends and family coming to say good-bye. This man is deeply loved and admired.

Wednesday, April 25—I was blessed in a precious way. Bob has not spoken in three days. He stopped eating and drinking some time ago. His mouth gets so dry, and no amount of moist swabbing seems to help. At one point I stood by his bedside kissing his face, arms, hands. I said, "I love you, Mr. Noonan. You are the love of my life." He got a soft, sweet smile on his face and said, "Love of my life." Words for me to treasure forever.

Thursday, April 26—Many visitors, many tears, many laughs, many remembrances. In the middle of the night, two aides came in for Bob's care as they had been doing every few hours. You could tell by his body language he was not happy when they disturbed him. This time aide Margaret said, "Mr. Bob, we have to take care of you now." He responded clearly, "No, no, no, no, no." The women finished their task and Margaret asked, "Mr. Bob, are you mad at me?" Again he spoke, clear as a bell, "Yes." "Well, how long are you going to be mad at me?" He replied, "Two hours." Margaret said, "Then I'm out of here." Two hours later she came back and asked, "Mr. Bob, are you still mad me?" He distinctly said, "No." We chuckled with sacred relief from the pain, suffering, and daily sacrifice as we received the gifts of Bob's forgiveness and wittiness. (Little did we know those words would be his last.)

Saturday, April 28—Our beloved Irishman died yesterday at 8:05 a.m.

PRAYER: *I thank you, Lord God, for the love of my life. May he find perfect bliss in your eternal glory. Amen.*

THOUGHT FOR THE DAY: Nothing—not even death—can separate us from God's love.

TORNADO TURMOIL

READ PSALM 130.

Out of the depths I cry to you, LORD;
Lord, hear my voice.
Let your ears be attentive
to my cry for mercy.
PSALM 130:1-2, NIV

On Tuesday, April 3, 2012, during Holy Week, my home church, Saint Barnabas United Methodist in Arlington, Texas, was hit by a vicious tornado. Staff scurried from the office building to the building next door to round up more than seventy preschoolers. They put them in an interior room, covered them with choir robes, and began singing and telling stories about Jesus. In a matter of minutes, roofs of buildings were blown off, windows were broken, there was extensive rain and water damage, and a huge uprooted tree was thrown upside-down by the sanctuary wall. But when the winds died, miraculously no one was hurt. The neighborhood surrounding the church suffered terrible damage, as did other areas in Dallas-Fort Worth hit by tornadoes that day. Bob and I, along with residents of our retirement community, were safely evacuated to the basement. The day was long—disruptive in mind and spirit and hard to comprehend. Yet we received lots of phone calls to check on us, and we felt loved.

Good Friday services were held in a neighborhood church, but I did not attend. Bob was weaker, more confused, and needed more assistance with everything. His best friend, Richard, came and sat with him Saturday afternoon while I went to the museum with a friend. He phoned later to say that he had seen a big change and that Bob was in decline. I even had to feed Bob his supper that night. Imagine my surprise when he got up Sunday morning and wanted to go to

Easter services that were being held in a neighborhood high school auditorium. He even instructed me to get out the purple shirt he had worn to granddaughter Ellen's wedding.

Our church buildings were devastated, but the church family was alive and thriving. The auditorium was filled with people—standing room only—glorious music, and joyful worship. The outpouring of gifts from sources near and far was astounding. The church traditionally held a huge Easter egg hunt for the neighborhood, and when word got out that all those plastic eggs, candy, and baskets were lost, other churches offered thousands of candy-filled eggs and hundreds of empty baskets for an enormous egg hunt on the football field. Bob was smiling, yet I could sense how tired he was. I had begun to question my ability to carry on, so I kept telling myself to fear not, fret not, walk in victory and love, and live each day with the spirit of the Resurrection.

Bob never got back to church; he died on April 27. The tornado turmoil left me without a church for his celebration of life service. It took days to get the time and place settled, which held up the obituary because I needed to include that information. Finally all was set for Memorial Day, a long and difficult month later. A resurrected Lord, a caring church staff, loving family and friends, and the kindness of a church congregation a mile away helped me walk in Easter victory.

PRAYER: *Risen Christ, you are in the world today. All around me I see manifestations of your loving care. You hear my cries, fill every need, and comfort my broken heart. I will sing eternal alleluias to you, my Redeemer King. Amen.*

THOUGHT FOR THE DAY: We walk in victory and love with the risen Christ.

I HEAR BOB CALLING

Read 1 Samuel 3:1-10.

The Lord came and stood there, calling as before,
"Samuel! Samuel!" And Samuel said, "Speak, for your
servant is listening."

1 Samuel 3:10

It happened again last night. About 2:00 a.m. I heard the call, "Nell, Nell, Nell." I jumped out of bed and dashed down the hallway into Bob's office. The voice was that of my husband when he needed help. *Had he fallen again? Was he having a panic attack?* I paused at the doorway and looked. He wasn't there—not on the floor, not in his big desk chair. My heart pounded. I heard him distinctly calling me. And then I remembered he had died three weeks earlier.

I suppose this is part of normal grief work, but I have had trouble getting back to sleep every time it happens. Back in bed, the tears came afresh when I thought how I would never hear my husband's real voice again. Gone are those wonderful breakfast prayers when he would say, "Good morning, Father God, Brother Jesus, and Holy Spirit; we adore you and praise you." I miss hearing thank you all day long as I brought meals and helped in any way. I miss his deep bass voice belting out hymns and old pop songs from his immense repertoire of lyrics. The stark, awful reality is our conversations have ended.

Hearing Bob's voice in the middle of the night brought to mind the story of Samuel who lived during the eleventh century BCE. Before his birth, his mother, Hannah, had consecrated him to the service of God, and so while he was still young, he went to live in the tabernacle at Shiloh with the chief priest Eli. One night Samuel, still a child, was lying asleep when he heard his name called, and he got up and went to Eli and said, "Here I am, for you called me" (1 Sam.

3:5). Eli told Samuel that he did not call him and to go back to bed. This scenario was repeated several times until Eli realized it was the Lord calling, and he told Samuel how to respond. So when the Lord came and called the young lad by name again, Samuel said, "Speak, for your servant is listening."

The story of Samuel's call from the Lord in the middle of the night reminds me that God wants me to cultivate a listening ear to hear God's voice. Time in scripture study, meditation, and prayer each day will open my heart to hear God's words of comfort, strength, wisdom, and healing. No matter how much hurt, disappointment, and bereavement I feel at any particular moment, God invites me to listen—even in times when there is no voice. The prophet Elijah sought the Lord and found God not in earthquake, wind, fire, but in a "still small voice" (1 Kings 19:12, KJV) or in "a sound of sheer silence" (NRSV). Bob's voice in the middle of the night was a reminder to sit quietly each day and listen.

PRAYER: *Father God, Brother Jesus, Holy Spirit, I believe you speak to me continually through scripture, your servants, creation, and life experiences that include grief. May I hear your voice in the quiet as well as in the noises of life. Speak, for your servant is listening. Amen.*

THOUGHT FOR THE DAY: God speaks in the silence; we must take time to listen.

IN MEMORIAM

READ JOB 19:25-27.

*I know that my Redeemer lives
and that at the last he will stand upon the earth.
After my awaking, he will raise me up;
and in my body I shall see God.
I myself shall see, and my eyes behold him
who is my friend and not a stranger.*

JOB 19:25-27, BCP

The above quotation comes from the opening section of the burial service I used for my personal good-bye when I took Bob's ashes to the bluebonnet field on Willow City loop near Fredericksburg, Texas, on August 9, 2012.

At the heart of the book of Job, Job offers his ringing affirmation of confidence: "I know that my Redeemer lives." Job thinks God has brought all those disasters upon him, yet he still expects to see God. In spite of his miserable situation, Job says, "In my body I shall see God." He is confident that God's justice will triumph, even if it will take a miracle like resurrection to accomplish it. This belief is so strong that Job becomes one of the first to talk about the resurrection of the body.

Like Job, even when faced with decay and death, Bob firmly believed that God would be on his side and he would behold God "face to face." He differed from Job in one major way: Bob never, ever, in all those years of chronic pain and suffering, blamed God for even one second of his misery and misfortunes. His faith was remarkable and inspirational. And so it was not surprising that the staff and members of Saint Barnabas United Methodist Church helped me and Bob's family hold a special service to celebrate the life of our beloved Irishman.

Because of the complication of finding a church since ours was destroyed by a tornado, the service took place a full month after Bob's death. It was tough nonetheless. The whole day was a bit of a blur, but I remember choking back tears and simply soldiering on. Scriptures were read, and prayers offered. Rev. Dr. Luther Henry, whom Bob had labeled "my brother," gave a moving homily. Bob used this moniker often, and it was humorous because Dr. Henry is African American. Bob especially enjoyed identifying him as his brother for the benefit of nurses or doctors who restricted visitors to family members only.

A musician offered an incredible vocal and piano worship tribute during a video of Bob's life composed by daughter-in-law Alice from a large collection of photographs. "When Irish Eyes Are Smiling" was selected for the postlude, but for some reason the musician decided to play it on the organ. My children began to chuckle as I apologized, "I'm sorry about that, Mr. Noonan. I know you hate organ music. I didn't know he was going to do that."

When I went into the room where the reception was held, I knew all was forgiven. The table was decorated with a green and white centerpiece, and glittery shamrocks were scattered among platters of Bob's favorites—mini cream puffs and mini chocolate éclairs—plus other goodies made by members of our Sojourners Sunday school class. The Irish theme was carried out with green napkins and a huge bowl of green punch. People stayed a long time laughing, crying, and remembering.

Bob was proficient in Latin. In memoriam and in my exhaustion, all I thought about when it finally ended was *Soli Deo gloria*—"glory to God alone."

PRAYER: *Redeemer God, I pray to you for those I love but see no longer. Grant them peace. Deal graciously with all who mourn that we may know the consolation of your love. Amen.*

THOUGHT FOR THE DAY: God offers consolation of love to those who mourn.

A COVENANT OF PEACE

READ ISAIAH 54:8-10.

---

*For the mountains may depart
and the hills be removed,
but my steadfast love shall not depart from you,
and my covenant of peace shall not be removed.*

ISAIAH 54:10

The ten-hour drive to south Mississippi from Fort Worth went smoothly, except for the sad fact that I would be attending our grandson's high-school graduation without Bob. I stopped and ate dinner with my remarkable mother at her retirement home before reaching my destination at the lake house of my brother and his wife.

Mikey, the cat, a sixteen-year-old feline, extremely thin due to hypothyroidism, woke me early that morning with his loud, persistent, humanlike cries. Years ago he had strayed up to Mike's back door, became his namesake, and has enjoyed my brother's protective care ever since. The cries became louder. After a vigorous petting and a bowl of food, he quieted down and sat quietly on the porch, observing the birds visiting the feeders. I settled into one of the rockers with a mug of steaming coffee.

There was a mist swirling gently above the lake, then ascending slowly and vanishing as the sun's rays became brighter in the new day. I observed the transformation in the watery reflections of the trees as they grew taller and greener with the rising sun. The setting was serene, and I felt the joy of nature deep within the recesses of my soul. It was a restorative place to be.

My brother and his wife were away, and the solitude provided a comforting respite from the twenty-two days since my husband died. The busyness of finding a church for his memorial service, designing the service and bulletin, getting the obituary in the newspaper, going to the Social Security office, and the myriad other details demanding immediate attention had taken a toll on my peace of mind. His death seemed to have set off a series of tectonic shifts with the earth's crust moving under my feet and leaving a series of aftershocks. Sitting there in silence, I could rest and lose myself in God's gifts of the natural world.

A rupture in the rhythm of life has been a common experience for God's people throughout history. That was exactly how I felt—the rhythm of my life had been ruptured. I found comfort in hymns about God's promises of restoration found in the book of Isaiah. The prophet reminds the people in exile in Babylon that God made an eternal covenant with Noah never again to destroy the earth by flood. God's promises are eternal and valid. The covenant of peace, mentioned in the scripture I selected for this devotion, signifies God's lasting commitment to be present with *steadfast love* permanently. The mountains and the tectonic plates may shift, but God shall never leave us. God's presence offers a holy harmony and peace even in the midst of tears.

PRAYER: *Compassionate God, I am grateful for the promise that you will be with me always. Even when my world is shifting, you hold me in steadfast love and permanent haven. Amen.*

THOUGHT FOR THE DAY: God's love for us is eternal.

MOPEY MOLLY

READ PSALM 102:1-5, 25-26.

My heart is blighted and withered like grass;
I forget to eat my food.

PSALM 102:4, NIV

She took up her post on the end of her master's bed, head down, sad eyes staring at the door of his bedroom, waiting for his return. It broke my heart to watch the pretty little Sheltie Bob had rescued nine years earlier. Except for walks, she had been the constant companion of this kind man who treated her like a princess. Did she understand somehow that he had been moved from our apartment to the hospice wing of the retirement community where we resided? Molly's vigil continued. She stopped eating; her water bowl stayed full.

Four days passed, and Bob died. As if on cue, Molly relocated to his bathroom, a place she had never gone before. It was tomblike, dark, windowless, with a cold stone tile floor. Reluctantly she came out for walks. Molly began to chew on her backside until a big, raw ulcer appeared. Her despondency was deep and relentless. As another week went by, I became more alarmed and took her to the veterinarian. A cortisone shot didn't relieve Molly's mopey behavior nor stop the chewing on her backside with its enlarging, hairless spot.

I told my neighbor and a number of residents about Molly's profound grief. Kaye said she wanted to come see her furry friend, and she coaxed Molly to sit with her on the sofa with the little dog's head in her lap. As I retreated to my bedroom to pray, I heard Kaye's soothing voice whisper, "Bob is gone, but it is going to be okay, Molly." About an hour after Kaye left, Molly emerged from Bob's bathroom, went to her food bowl, and ate every morsel.

One of Bob's dying concerns was the well-being of his little dog. He made me promise I would take good care of her. I breathed a sigh of relief that she was eating and pulling out of her despair. However, it was premature. Molly returned to the bathroom after our evening walk and began chewing at the base of her tail. The mopes were back with a vengeance. *If only I could soothe her worries and help her grief,* I thought. But I was helpless and immersed in my own sadness, which didn't help matters for my sensitive, furry companion.

Molly went to be boarded while I drove out of state to attend grandchildren's high-school graduations. I came back to a perkier little dog. But after a day in the apartment, Molly resumed her journey of grief, although she did continue to eat. How long will the overwhelming struggle with the loss of our beloved Irishman go on? Is God listening to my prayers for relief? How long will it hurt so much? I wish I had some answers, but the truth is I don't know. In the meantime Molly and I must hold on with a raggedy hope that Kaye's words are inspired prophecy: "Bob is gone, but it is going to be okay."

PRAYER: *Gracious and loving God, thank you for bringing friends of faith to accompany me through the deeps of dark sadness and bewildering grief. Grant me strength for the journey. Amen.*

THOUGHT FOR THE DAY: God's friends provide us with courage and strength for living.

PUDDLES OF GRIEF

Read Psalm 23.

Even though I walk through the darkest valley,
I fear no evil;
for you are with me;
your rod and your staff—
they comfort me.

Psalm 23:4

Episodes of grief continue to pop up unexpectedly. One occurred last night when I was eating my supper of stuffed peppers and corn on the cob. My husband appreciated the simple pleasures of fresh food and my home-cooked efforts, and he especially enjoyed this particular summertime meal. He would slather his corn with generous amounts of butter, salt, and coarse ground pepper. We would hold hands while he said grace, and then he quickly chomped down and began to savor every drippy mouthful. The recollection of a simple man enjoying a simple meal had me simply dripping in buttery tears last night.

I am not sure what the trigger was this morning, but I stumbled into another puddle of grief while I was doing my daily devotions. I miss my sweetheart and long to converse with him, to tell him what I'm doing and thinking, to hear his deep voice respond and tell me his thoughts and feelings. The sharing of little mundane comments and running commentary of daily life are gone. The loss—the silence— is irreversible and permanent. I've heard several widowed men and women remark that conversation with the beloved is the thing they miss the most.

In two weeks, I leave to go in search of a new home near my daughter and my sister. The rent on a spacious apartment in this wonderful retirement community is high for a single person, and

I made the decision a month ago to move. The time has seemed like an eternity with mourning and waiting. I should be sorting and organizing. And there's the matter of Bob's clothes. Some days I lose myself in missing my sweetheart. I guess it's normal right now to go and do something and then hit another puddle of grief. I remember words of advice from a grief counselor: "Be kind to yourself. Have patience and trust the process."

Millions of people in dark, scary, lonely spaces through the centuries have found solace and encouragement in the words of the Good Shepherd Psalm (a favorite I memorized in third grade). "For you are with me; your rod and your staff—they comfort me." I am learning to "trust the process," but in the meantime, I plan to buy some of those flashy, flowery galoshes for my new home in North Carolina and for surprising little puddles of tears.

PRAYER: *Lord God of life and death, when I recall the passing of my loved one, I feel such a sense of loss. You remind me that love reaches beyond the touch of death. For that blessed comfort I give thanks. Amen.*

THOUGHT FOR THE DAY: Love reaches beyond the touch of death.

FEARS, FLEAS, AND FRIENDS

Read Isaiah 41:9-13.

I am the LORD your God
who takes hold of your right hand
and says to you, Do not fear;
I will help you.

Isaiah 41:13, NIV

Three months after Bob died, I remember sitting in my bedroom armchair and suddenly bursting into tears. When the tears ebbed, I asked myself about the feelings behind that rush of grief. Journaling helped with an insight: I felt vulnerable, insecure, and afraid. For years, the management of our household, finances, and medical needs had fallen on my shoulders, but somehow I had lost confidence in my abilities without Bob's presence. I felt like a wounded animal that wanted to hide away—exactly what our dog Molly had done when she sought refuge in Bob's bathroom.

I knew I would face huge questions and transitions in the future—Where would I move? When? Would I have enough funds? How would I manage if I got sick? What if I made the wrong decisions? How was I going to take care of business when I felt so tired and sad all the time? The darkness grew darker and the sighs of my heart grew deeper. My time seemed so empty without Bob. Empty space tends to create fear, and I was letting fear fill the corners of my life. I wallowed in my fears and listened to the gravelly groans of my gut for a couple of hours.

I read a story recently that described those dreadful feelings of vulnerability and grief. Flora Slosson Wuellner included the story in an article titled "Feast and Fear" in *Weavings: A Journal of the Christian Spiritual Life.* * A woman had rescued an abandoned, frightened, young dog whose abusers had tried to drown him. His wounds needed to be cleaned, but when she tried to lower the dog into a warm tub, he fought with all his might. He was terrified and his body stiffened with fear. The woman could think of only one way to reach him. She stripped to her underwear and got into the tub with all the fleas, dirt, and blood. She stroked him gently, talked to him quietly and held him until he began to relax, and she was able to clean the wounds. Then the healing could begin. This amazing story reminded Wuellner (and now me) of the Incarnation and the way God deals with our resistance, our fears, our wounds: God climbs in with us.

We need not fear because God has established a relationship with us. God gives us assurance of help and victory over sin, death, vulnerability, fears—and even fleas. God is friend; Jesus is friend; Spirit is friend.

PRAYER: *Incarnating God, redeeming Son, comforting Spirit: thank you for finding me when I am in the grip of dark fear and for taking my hand and leading me into the light. Amen.*

THOUGHT FOR THE DAY: Do not fear; God is with us always.

Weavings 27, no. 3 (May/June/July 2012): 7.

FATHER'S DAY

READ PSALMS 22 AND 23.

Though I walk through the valley of the shadow of death,
I will fear no evil;
For You are with me.

PSALM 23:4, NKJV

I planned to attend the Fort Worth Writers' session this morning, but as I began my devotional time, I had a major meltdown. I simply had to yield to it. The wave of grief, the rush of tears, the brokenness of my heart took over and made the change in plans for me.

I feel lost without my husband. Every evening we watched local and world news, and we never missed the televised Texas Rangers games. Last night I was all by myself—without Bob. There was no small talk and commentary, no deep laughter when I jumped up, clapped, and danced at the home runs and great plays. When Bob and I watched the games together, he was amused at my antics and playfulness, and he would flash me one of those signature smiles. Life feels strange without him, and I miss him.

As I approach the Father's Day weekend, I am feeling my grief more acutely. Even regular Sundays are difficult, but this one, coming seven weeks after his death, is especially bittersweet. Bob loved his two children and three stepchildren and felt some responsibility for them even during his health crises. On Wednesday I sent Father's Day cards to the three sons like the two of us had always done, and I know they will feel a tug at their hearts too. My children get an extra whammy because they lost their biological father as well as their beloved stepdad this year.

I feel better after experiencing a full-blown cry with runny, red nose and deep weeping. It helped. Turning back to my devotions, I read Psalm 22, the Psalm of the Cross, containing the quote of Jesus: "My God, My God, why have You forsaken Me?" (v. 1, NKJV). This psalm has no still waters, no green pastures, no oil of gladness. Jesus' cry from the cross opens up the dark aloneness at the core of our lives. It is after the yielding and acceptance of the shadowy sadness of death, the stripping back to the bones of our existence, that we can fully appreciate the psalm that follows the twenty-second.

The Twenty-third Psalm, called the Good Shepherd Psalm, is set in green pastures alongside still waters where nothing is lacking. The One who can walk with us through death's dark valley will lead us safely to the other side. Notice how personal the Shepherd becomes in the depths of darkness. "The LORD *is* my shepherd" (v. 1, NKJV). There are seventeen personal pronouns: makes *me*, leads *me,* restores *me,* guides *me, my* head, *my* cup, and more.

The direct intimacy of this psalm brought instant comfort to my mourning today. The Shepherd was alongside me as a companion walking not just in the sadness but *through* the dark valley and *beyond* to the banquet table and the overflowing cup. The promise seeps into the recesses of my soul and brings hope. "Surely goodness and mercy shall follow me all the days of my life; and I will dwell in the house of the LORD forever" (Ps. 23:6, NKJV).

PRAYER: *Father God, you bless your children with the hope of restoration and safe haven no matter the circumstances of their lives. What a priceless Father's Day gift! I am beyond grateful. Amen.*

THOUGHT FOR THE DAY: The Good Shepherd walks alongside us through the dark valley.

IN-BETWEEN TIMES

READ ISAIAH 43:1-4.

When you pass through the waters, I will be with you;
and through the rivers, they shall not overwhelm you.

ISAIAH 43:2

Ten weeks after Bob's death, I traveled to a retreat house in Houston, Texas, for eight days of silence broken only by one hour of daily counsel and worship. The grief counselor invited me to enter my sadness as deeply as I could. I cried, I sobbed, I thrashed about in the waters of my grief for three days. Then she asked me to remember things I was grateful for in my marriage and to journal my thanksgivings for what my husband and I had together.

By day five, the heaviness had lifted a bit, and I seemed to be emerging from the depths of interior darkness. After a nice walk and a scrumptious supper of fish and fresh asparagus, I sat outdoors in a swing and watched birds darting to and from the feeder. A peacock and a peahen foraged for insects in the tall grass. Little breaks in the clouds offered patches of blue through the gray skies. My tranquility was abruptly shattered when I noticed some statuary in a corner of the garden: a boy and a girl sitting among the flowers facing each other. A wave of grief hit. My peacock, my boy, my mate is gone. I cried and later had trouble sleeping.

The next morning I sat in one of the rockers, drinking a second mug of coffee and watching a sole mourning dove. Back in my room, I wrote this poem:

In-Between Times
She sits in an old porch rocking chair;
Cradles a mug of hot coffee.

Watches a feathered intruder
On the pea gravel pathway

Persistent, fervent, plaintive dove coos
pierce the dawn's hush.
The mate does not respond;
He, his cuddles, gone forever.

Widow eyes leak deep, silent
tears of lonely woundedness.
Pleading release from
ripped-apart heart.

Patiently, impatient she waits . . .
for the sadness to soften,
for the Lord to mold mourning into morning,
for whispers of resurrection.
She waits . . .

PRAYER: *Lord of compassion, grieving is such hard, uncomfortable, neces-sary work. I know I cannot force or hurry the journey. Thank you for being with me as I simply abide in-between mourning and morning. Amen.*

THOUGHT FOR THE DAY: We wait on the Lord to turn mourning into morning.

IN THE MOMENT

READ PSALM 42.

Why are you cast down, O my soul,
and why are you disquieted within me?
Hope in God; for I shall again praise him,
my help and my God.

PSALM 42:11

Dadgumit, here it comes again!

I had tricked myself into thinking I was making huge strides in healing after my husband's death, but this morning the tears were flowing. A memory had popped up suddenly while I was reading some meditations by a hospital chaplain. What I remembered vividly was my little family huddled in the hall, all of us weeping, deeply grieved, as we watched the gurney with Bob's body bag being rolled from the hospice room to the elevator. The pain pierced my heart to its core. In that moment, I felt frozen by intense, excruciating loss.

The fresh tears today remind me there are no slapdash shortcuts through grief. We cannot force the process. In this moment, my soul is disquieted, cast down, like that of the psalmist. I enter a time of grief and simply abide there for a while, honoring the memory of my husband's death, the shared love, and my own bereavement. Grief is what it is.

The psalmist does not simply state the facts of a soul in struggle and mourning but goes on to envision a future in which God restores hope and renewed life. We too can exercise such hope and praise. Making a new, free, happy life is a work of art. In the moment, I have a keen awareness that transformation occurs only through heartrending struggle. Yet our moments of grief and struggle are just that—moments. They don't last. We live in them, change comes, and we move on. The God of our past and the God of our future is here, wherever the moment finds us.

PRAYER: *Encouraging, reassuring God, give me courage and perseverance to seek your will and to follow where you lead, even when I don't know where I am going. Amen.*

THOUGHT FOR THE DAY: Christ calls us to new hope and life.

BLUEBONNET BENEDICTION

READ ISAIAH 35:1-10.

The desert and the parched land will be glad;
the wilderness will rejoice and blossom.
Like the crocus, it will burst into bloom;
it will rejoice greatly and shout for joy. . . .
Gladness and joy will overtake them,
and sorrow and sighing will flee away.

ISAIAH 35:1-2, 10, NIV

There was a knock at the door of Lillie Marlene Cottage, a charming bed-and-breakfast where I was staying overnight in Fredericksburg, Texas. The owner, an attractive, soft-spoken woman named Marlene Pylate, said, "I know you are here to take your husband's ashes to the bluebonnet field as he requested. I would be humbled if you would let me accompany you. I don't want to intrude, but I know exactly the place you describe, and this is an emotional time for you."

At eight o'clock the morning of August 9, 2012, Marlene drove me with the black box bearing Bob's ashes to Willow City Loop. The Texas hill country has a unique beauty of rugged, rocky hills, mesquite trees, and plump clumps of prickly pear cacti. A flood of memories poured forth as I remembered when Bob and I had journeyed to this holy ground and sacred space. Marlene found the dry creek bed—the cattle gap—the spot Bob found so enchanting. We called it "a thin place," a place where heaven and earth meet, where the veil is lifted for a little glimpse of the heart and face of God.

Marlene and I found some shade under a large mesquite tree several yards from the road. I read the "Burial of the Dead, Rite 2" from my small, black Book of Common Prayer that is falling apart like my heart:

Happy from now on
are those who die in the Lord!
So it is, says the Spirit,
for they rest from their labors.

Scripture readings from Isaiah, the Revelation of John, and the Gospel of John followed. "Give rest, O Christ, to your servant Bob with your saints, *where sorrow and pain are no more, neither sighing, but life everlasting,*" I recited. I spread Bob's ashes there on the dry creek bank where bluebonnets would bloom profusely in the spring, turning the parched land into indescribable rivers of deep blue. "We commit Bob's body to the ground; earth to earth, ashes to ashes, dust to dust. The Lord bless him and keep him . . . and give him peace. Amen."

After Marlene and I departed and were a few yards down the road toward the car, we saw three young raccoons playing on some rocks. When we reached the car and started the ignition, two deer were startled and ran off into the brush. Marlene said, "You know about the animals, don't you? I believe they are filled with Bob's spirit, and they are thanking you for bringing him to this holy place and saying that he will be okay here—never hurting and never alone. I will send you a picture in April." I am eternally grateful for her benediction.

My rite of passage for Bob was a God-filled experience where heaven "came down." My grieving heart has been massaged by humility, hope, and holiness.

PRAYER: *"Almighty God, Father of mercies and giver of comfort: Deal graciously, we pray, with all who mourn; that, casting all their care on you, they may know the consolation of your love; through Jesus Christ our Lord. Amen"* (BCP).

THOUGHT FOR THE DAY: God comforts and consoles with everlasting love.

OUT OF CONTROL

READ JEREMIAH 29:11-13.

*"I know the plans I have for you," declares the LORD, "plans
to prosper you and not to harm you, plans to give you hope
and a future. Then you will call on me and come and pray
to me, and I will listen to you."*

JEREMIAH 29:11-12, NIV

I am falling apart today; I feel out of control. My mind jumps from one thought to another like a bed full of monkeys, and I'm the one who fell off and bumped my head. I want to scream, "Mama, call the doctor," while seriously doubting anyone can help me. A hurting soul cannot be satisfied with quick fixes.

My husband died four months ago, and it stings worse today than it did then. During more than seven years of caregiving, I engaged in some slow, steady, anticipatory grief. I was shocked by his death but also relieved that he no longer suffered so horribly. All persons' experiences are unique to them, and I've been told by good friends that a sudden, unexpected loss is quite different from my journey. But we do have something in common: pain and grief and disorientation. We fell off and bumped our heads.

It is an inelegant, confusing process, this process called grief. Today I don't feel useful anymore. I have relinquished my need to do anything purposeful, to succeed at anything, to impress anyone—including God. I must have packed my courage and work ethic in a suitcase that got lost in the airport baggage claim. Is this emptiness what Jesus means when he talks about the "poor in spirit"? Is this poverty of soul formed in my heartrending struggle part of a transformative work preparing me to receive God and God's will for the rest of my days on earth? I live with so many questions and no answers. I suppose I simply need to quit mewling, be patient with the bereavement process, and let God work out my future. But right now I just want two aspirin for my bumped head.

When feeling confused, stressed, or out of control, I go to my bedroom and sit in my overstuffed armchair. This morning I wasn't even conscious I was doing that, and I'm not sure how long I had been sitting there. Out of habit, I reached for my Bible and my *Disciple* study manual and started to read. The brain fog began to lift as I read and re-read Jeremiah's letter to the exiles in Babylon. He tells them to pray for their captors and to move ahead with their lives. He reminds them that life cannot grind to a halt during troubled times or distressing and difficult circumstances. He gives clear instructions in the letter (see Jeremiah 29:4-23) to pray diligently and do whatever they can rather than give up because of fear, uncertainty, tribulation, and grief. Jeremiah relays the message that God has not forgotten God's people. God's plans for their future are good and full of hope. This does not mean they will be spared pain, suffering, or hardship but that God will see them through to a glorious conclusion.

That letter was for me. My future is in God's hands; God has not forgotten me. I need to go to God in prayer again and again until my scary, out-of-control spells pass. In prayer time, something mysterious happens. God wipes away fear and brings peace to my troubled spirit. Little monkey, please trust God, and, for heaven's sake, stop jumping on the bed.

PRAYER: *Merciful God, forgive me when I fail to trust you to guide and provide for my future. Thank you for bringing peace to my troubled mind and heart. Amen.*

THOUGHT FOR THE DAY: We trust God's plans for the future.

NOT READY YET

READ MATTHEW 6:9-13.

"Pray then in this way:
Our Father in heaven,
hallowed be your name.
Your kingdom come.
Your will be done,
on earth as it is in heaven."

MATTHEW 6:9-10

I sat next to Edith's bed and held her frail hand in mine. I said a personal prayer and then went right into reciting the prayer Jesus taught his disciples. The dying woman began mouthing the words with me and her family. This is a prayer deeply embedded in Christians. People of all ages and stages of faith become community during the recitation of The Lord's Prayer. "Your kingdom come. Your will be done." Together, for a moment, we hope in God's glorious dream, God's powerful vision for the world.

There is scarcely a page in the synoptic Gospels (Matthew, Mark, Luke) without a reference to the kingdom of God, the reign of God, or the reign of heaven. When Mark recounts the first appearance of Jesus after his forty days in the wilderness, he records, "Now after John was arrested, Jesus came to Galilee, proclaiming the good news of God, and saying, 'The time is fulfilled, and the kingdom of God has come near; repent, and believe in the good news'" (1:14-15). From that point on, the kingdom is the central theme in the preaching and life of Jesus. He upholds the Jewish belief that God's goal is the wholeness and completion of creation, while going beyond it. He not only preaches the kingdom but also ties its coming to his own person and to his ministry. He is the authentic, effective instrument God uses to bring about the fulfillment of the kingdom.

I reflected on that many times today as I thought about Edith and all persons experiencing death and the loss of a loved one. Five months have passed since Bob died, and I have been reading back over my journals. They are packed with expressions of mourning, grief, tears, feeling adrift, awareness of areas of pain not ready yet for change or healing. The flow of prayer shows me God's love is not assaulting me with charges to "get over it and move on." It is enough just to grieve for a while and imagine Christ gently touching the fear and pain buried so deep that I am not consciously hearing the cries of my hidden emotions and thoughts. I'm not yet ready to go there and look at them.

I am functioning well in my outer life, but in the secret recesses of my being, I feel messy and sad. I yearn for healing to penetrate the depths of my being. I hold the hope that the risen Lord will guide me out of the shadows while also sensing a need to stay inside the transforming cocoon for a while longer. The time required to emerge from deep grief will be different for each of us. God understands and will stay beside us—Edith, you, me, all of us—as we journey through our time of mourning.

PRAYER: *Loving God of compassion and mercy, I pray for your help in being patient in grief, faithful in prayer, and joyful in hope. I pray for release from self-preoccupation with my grief so that I may find increased opportunities to participate in the building of your kingdom come. Amen.*

THOUGHT FOR THE DAY: Prayer is one source of daily support during both good and dark times.

FULLNESS OF JOY

Read John 16:19-24.

*"So you have pain now; but I will see you again, and your
hearts will rejoice, and no one will take your joy from you. . . .
Ask and you will receive, so that your joy may be complete."*

John 16:22, 24

I hadn't laughed that way in weeks—what a glorious feeling! The
members of my Sunday school class had spent most of the hour telling
"Bob stories." They held a deep affection for the old Irishman and
were remembering some of his amusing antics. It all started when
one of them said he was going to eat a blueberry doughnut in Bob's
memory, which brought a quick retort that, in that case, he better eat
two. Another friend told about the time Bob wheeled his motorized
chair up to a minister who was leaving to accept a call to another
ministry, shook the pastor's hand, and wished him Godspeed. Then
came Bob's confession: "I understand you are a very good preacher,
but I wouldn't know. I've slept through every one of your sermons."

As if right on cue, another class member spilled a cup of coffee,
again "in Bob's honor." We all laughed and remembered how we sat on
alert to help prevent Bob's spills, but somehow he managed to sneak
one in almost every Sunday. (His neuropathy had numbed most of
the feeling in his hands.) These brothers and sisters in Christ loved
their friend so much they would tease and salve away any embarrass-
ment. Our relationships embodied the fellowship of the church at
its best—a truly Christlike support group. The stories and laughter
brought spontaneous relief to my grieving soul. I felt grateful.

For decades I've begun the day by reciting the morning daily
devotion found in the Book of Common Prayer, and today I was
reminded of one of the lines from Psalm 51: "Give me the joy of your

saving help again and sustain me with your bountiful Spirit" (v. 13). That petition was granted today; joy wrapped her arms around me through the presence of caring friends.

The scriptures are filled with words like *joy, joyous, joyful, joyfully, overjoyed, jubilant,* and *jubilation.* Psalm 68:3 states "Let [the righteous] be jubilant with joy." In the eighth chapter of the book of Nehemiah, the priest Ezra opens the book of the law of Moses and reads to the people who have returned from Babylonian exile: "This day is holy to our LORD; and do not be grieved, for the joy of the LORD is your strength" (v. 10). These scriptures serve as loving reminders that God does not ask me to stop laughing just because my husband died.

A friend added one of those little insert cards in a note that reads, "Do not weep for what is gone but laugh because it happened." Another friend told me he liked what someone told him when his wife died: "Cry until you laugh and laugh until you cry." I'm not fond of pithy little sayings, but I think what these two and the scriptures are saying is God's love is boundless in good times and sad. God's love will carry us through times of tears until we reach a place of gratitude and praise for God's goodness. Julian of Norwich (ca. 1342–1416), an English mystic, wrote, "The fullness of joy is to behold God in everything." *Everything*—including our journey of grief. May it be so.

PRAYER: *God of compassion and steadfast goodness, I ask for your gift of joy that invites me to find laughter, hope, and healing even in my days of mourning. Amen.*

THOUGHT FOR THE DAY: God's love sustains us through times of tears.

BROKEN
AND
BLESSED

The spirit of the Lord GOD is upon me,
because the LORD has anointed me;
he has sent me to bring good news to the oppressed,
to bind up the brokenhearted . . .
to comfort all who mourn.

ISAIAH 61:1-2

ONE-YEAR ANNIVERSARY

Read Psalm 94:17-19.

When the cares of my heart are many,
your consolations cheer my soul.

Psalm 94:19

One year ago my husband died. At 8:07 a.m. at the beginning of the fifth day of vigil in the sparse hospice room, his shallow breathing stopped. Mystery simply came and enveloped him. My youngest son, Bill, had arrived, and we were quietly sitting together, sipping coffee from Styrofoam cups. The nurse came with her stethoscope and confirmed Bob had slipped away to his eternal delight with the Lord—an end to years and years of excruciating suffering and pain.

Bob was gone from us. We had time to prepare, but this experience was cataclysmic nonetheless. Bill slipped out of the room to go tell his wife and to give me time to smother my beloved's face and hands with kisses and to smooth down his hair and to whisper love's intimate words of devotion and farewell. Hospice called the other children, the church, and special designated friends.

I watched in silence as two women from hospice washed Bob's face and his entire limp body from head to toe and then rubbed it with lotion gently, respectfully, lovingly. I felt pulled in as if I were applying the lotion myself as part of the team. The work was holy, mysterious, yet the most validating and authentic task a human being could engage in this side of heaven. I thought about the women who return to the garden of Gethsemane to anoint Jesus' body with aromatic oils and prepare him for burial. But they are never able to begin the task. He lives!

Today as I recall and relive that day of sorrow, I look at my wedding album and a box of sympathy cards and letters. My heart still bears the stain of tears from that day of immense loss. This year of wilderness grief and tremendous transitions has been tough but has forged a deeper, softer heart that not only looks backward but also forward. I have a living treasure of amazing memories to nourish my life. I know that love is beyond the touch of death and that mine and Bob's love for each other remains eternally. God is good in life, good in death, good all the time.

And so I also look forward to the future with God holding, encouraging, comforting, and healing me and softening my sadness every day. Even when I was lost in grief, God found me. And now I am learning to internalize the gifts of love Bob and I shared and to take them with me as I create a new life.

PRAYER: *Compassionate Lord, be present with me as I await my final day on earth and grant eternal joy and peace to my beloved. Amen.*

THOUGHT FOR THE DAY: Even when lost in grief, God finds us.

COMFORT FOOD

READ JOHN 6:48-51.

---

*"I am the bread of life. Your ancestors ate the manna in the
wilderness, and they died. This is the bread that comes down
from heaven, so that one may eat of it and not die."*

JOHN 6:48-50

Six months after Bob's death, I moved to be near my daughter and
my sister in North Carolina. When one of my new neighbors learned I
am a retired librarian and widow, he introduced me to another widow
and university librarian who lives in our neighborhood. Although she
is much younger, we have the common bond of having lost husbands
plus we share our vocational experience. It turns out we enjoy many of
the same things including religious affiliation, a love of choral music,
an affinity for all things Celtic, and an appreciation of good food.

One night the two of us decided to go to dinner and a play. While
feasting on Italian cuisine, we shared stories about our husbands and
the way they enjoyed their food with gusto. The beauty of finding
a widow pal is that I have someone to talk with about my beloved
because she understands my need to do that. She listens, and then it's
her turn to remember and tell stories. Such a friendship is therapeutic
and important.

The conversation drifted to a behavior that began after Bob died. I
maintain a healthy diet all day and for supper. But somewhere around
nine in the evenings I crave munchies and sweets until I am so sleepy
I am forced to go to bed. Ice cream, tortilla strips and salsa, cookies,
popcorn, strawberries dipped in powdered sugar, and the list goes on.
A few pounds, plus additional inches on my waistline, showed up the
first year of widowhood. Clothes became snug. Sadly I simply didn't
care. My sweet neighbor looked at me with a huge grin on her face.

"I do that too, but my comfort food of choice is chocolate—any and all things chocolate."

The craving, the hunger, the stomach rumblings are only a longing for my absent spouse and a desire for his companionship again, especially after the sun goes down. Sadness, depression, and grief after such immense loss are involuntary responses, and they make life messy and bewildering. People keep telling me it will get better with time. The healing process does indeed take time. I am learning to accept the fact that my life is changed forever by my loss. This awful stage hurts—hurts terribly.

I am discovering this truth in the midst of the grieving process: I cannot rush through or avoid the desert of sadness and depression. I cannot go around, over, or under it; I must go through it. I am learning to embrace the difficult feelings and to reflect on my loss. Often I don't sense God's presence, but when I go deep into my inner sanctuary, at some point, I feel a nudge from God or hear the still, small voice letting me know God is with me every step of the way. Hope and healing are stirred anew. The Lord comes to sate my hunger, to work a miracle like that of the manna for the Israelites or the loaves and fishes for the five thousand. I find comfort food when I remember Jesus saying, "I am the bread of life."

PRAYER: *True God of hope and comfort, restore all of us who suffer in body, mind, or spirit with the power of your healing love. Thank you for your presence as I journey toward healing and new life. Amen.*

THOUGHT FOR THE DAY: God's steadfast presence brings comfort to our journey.

TEARS IN A BOTTLE

READ PSALM 56:8-13.

You have kept count of my tossings;
put my tears in your bottle.

PSALM 56:8

The words jumped off the page: "You . . . put my tears in your bottle."
Not only does God keep a record of times I toss and turn during my
fretful nights, God also collects my tears and fastidiously saves each
drop in a bottle. This impressive metaphor, expressing the depth of
God's concern for me, penetrated my sorrow like a bolt of lightning
piercing a dark sky. The idea the Lord cares and loves me enough to
catch my tears—and there have been many—in a bottle filled me with
comfort, healing, humility, and overflowing praise.

I read Psalm 56 again. It is an individual lament probably written
by King David when the Philistines held him in the city of Gath. He
speaks of enemies, malicious plots, and conspiracies. But David also
expresses confidence and a complete trust in God that wipes away
all fear: "In God I trust; I am not afraid" (v. 4). He pledges a thank
offering when his prayer is answered. "For you have delivered my soul
from death, and my feet from falling, so that I may walk before God
in the light of life" (v. 13).

I read the psalm a third time and began to cry. Tears are a fre-
quent companion, a natural reaction to grief. I read in a handout from
hospice that scientists have discovered tears of grief have a different
chemical makeup than tears from a physical injury. Crying during
a season of mourning releases toxins from the body and encourages
the healing process. And yet I seem to have bought into our cultural
discomfort with tears. Crying does not signify weakness, breaking
down, or losing it. Yet I hide my tears from the outside world and
weep in private where no one can see. I throw myself on my bed and

sob until my pillow is a soggy puddle of tears and my body is depleted of energy. The release and relief that follow such an episode bring comfort and solace to my broken heart. I feel purged, strengthened, and able to go forward again.

In a favorite little book titled *His Gifts to Me,* author Marie Chapian combines several scriptures in "The Gift of Tears" to form this anchoring message:

When you sow in tears,
    you will reap in joyful singing.
The grief and sorrows of today
    will not last,
for I comfort you
    in My embrace
and give to you the gift of tears,
    which I keep in bottles on My holy shelf.
    Nothing pertaining to you
escapes My gaze.
    When you cry, dear one,
give your tears to Me,
    where they are safe. *

My tears invite awareness that God is nearby, sharing fully in my humanity in all its sadness and blessedness.

PRAYER: *God of love and mercy, who knows the grief hidden within the depths of my heart, I give thanks for the gift of tears and for the knowledge that you care and that you are never far from me. Amen.*

THOUGHT FOR THE DAY: Let yourself have your healing tears; they are precious to God.

*Marie Chapian, *His Gifts to Me* (Minneapolis, MN: Bethany House Publishers, 1988). 172–3.

MIGHTY MITES

A poor widow came and put in two small copper coins,
which are worth a penny. . . . As [Jesus] came out of the
temple, one of his disciples said to him, "Look, Teacher,
what large stones and what large buildings!"

MARK 12:42; 13:1

Things that used to seem important don't seem to matter anymore—my heart, prayer, purpose, life, value, worth. As a relatively new widow, I felt empty and disoriented, even nauseated from deep grief. It's almost like being lost in some kind of non-world. I wish my life could go back to normal, whatever that is. I can't even remember what life was like before my husband got sick and died.

Looking for some emotional, spiritual anchor for the day, I faithfully opened my Bible and began the daily lectionary readings. In Mark 12, Jesus observes the people making contributions to the thirteen collection boxes in the Court of the Women for the daily sacrifices and expenses of the Temple. Many throw in sizable contributions. Then comes a poor widow who offers two mites, small copper coins. A mite is the smallest of all coins, worth only a small fraction of a denarius, or a day's wage, yet Jesus remarks her contribution is the greatest of all. The amount of the gift never matters as much as the cost to the giver. She recklessly gives all, not keeping back anything, not one single coin. Her financial future is insecure, and yet she trusts God to supply her every need.

Following this scenario with the poor widow, Jesus leaves the Temple, and one of his disciples expresses amazement at the size of the stones. Historian Josephus reports that some of these stones were forty feet long by twelve feet high by eighteen feet wide. The size of

A WIDOW'S PRAYER

55

the stones and buildings moves the Galilean disciple to express wonder and awe at such massive splendor and magnificence. Jesus sees this as a monument to greed and power paid by lives of the workers who built it and warns of the destruction to come. Nothing in the material world is so vast and solid that it will stand forever. The poor widow has it right. She reminds me that the only thing that really counts is the right relationship with God.

Widowhood brings on huge changes in income for many of us and adjustments in lifestyle follow. I sell things and a check comes, and somehow there is always enough in the bank account to fund the moving van, a new place to live, new tires for long drives, the church pledge. We may feel we do not have much in the way of material things or gifts to give to God, but in offering what we have, we learn to trust God to supply our every need. Jesus does not see the widow as somehow inferior, diminished, powerless, or as a valueless object. He gives witness to her faithful devotion to future generations.

Reading this lovely story makes me imagine Jesus coming before my droopy head, lifting up my chin, kissing me on the forehead, and telling me how precious all widows are in his sight.

PRAYER: *Generous and gracious God, thank you for your son who loves the "least of these" and gives them power, value, and blessing beyond their imaginings. Amen.*

THOUGHT FOR THE DAY: We can trust in God to supply our every need.

MOVING ON

READ GENESIS 12:1-9.

The LORD said to Abram, "Go from your country and your kindred and your father's house to the land that I will show you. I will make of you a great nation, and I will bless you, and make your name great, so that you will be a blessing."

GENESIS 12:1-2

Abram's (his name changes to Abraham in Genesis 17) family moves from Ur, an ancient city near the Euphrates River at the southern tip of Mesopotamia, to Haran, a city at the crossroads of major trade routes in northernmost Mesopotamia. After Abram's father, Terah, dies, God calls Abram and gives him travel directions to go to Canaan with promises of blessing to follow upon Abram's fulfillment of God's command. The complex history of the book of Genesis emphasizes God's covenants that bless and protect human beings who are expected to be obedient, to believe, and to have faith in God.

I thought about the amount of courage and trust required in order for Abram and other biblical heroes to follow God's commands. I felt intimidated by their example, but realized I needed that same strength to move on with my life as a widow both literally and figuratively. I felt God telling me to move from my Texas home to live in North Carolina to be near my daughter and my sister, but every time I would think about all that had to be done—the logistics of finding a new place to live, figuring out the finances, finding a commercial mover, organizing, packing, and driving two days with a dog—a wave of grief would hit me. Yesterday I walked Molly and then climbed back into bed and stayed there for hours.

There have been occasional breaks in the funk when I would get a few things done, but often I have felt emotionally taxed to the breaking point. I managed to quickly find places for all the medical equipment and supplies, but I postponed facing Bob's closet for months until I forced myself to tackle it today. I sorted and packed up all of Bob's clothes and took them to Goodwill. I say "all," but there was an exception: his purple shirt bought for granddaughter Ellen's wedding. He wore it only one other time and that was Easter Sunday, his last time to attend church. It hangs in the back of my closet; I'm not ready to let go yet. It has been an emotional day.

Moving on is such a hard thing to do. We face uncertainty and the loss of what we have known. My world as I knew it—and as I expected it to be—has been turned inside out, upside down. But I told Jesus years ago, "I want to follow you," so now I must summon up the courage and trust to act upon the faith I profess. Abram leaves his familiar land on a promise that God will provide. I too must get up and go, uncertain about my future as a new widow in a new place but certain that I am on the way to new blessings with God.

PRAYER: *My Lord and my God, hear my prayer for courage and faith as I prepare to move on with my life. Be my companion and my guide every step of the journey. Amen.*

THOUGHT FOR THE DAY: Wherever we go, God goes with us.

BUMPY BOAT RIDE

READ MARK 6:45-51.

Immediately [Jesus] spoke to [the disciples] and said, "Take heart, it is I; do not be afraid."

MARK 6:50

One morning I was sitting in my favorite chair for prayers and devotions when I felt overwhelmed by the difficulties of so many transitions and changes in my life. The trigger for my angst came from my attempt the previous afternoon to get a car tag in the state where I had moved to be near family after my husband's death. I had to take the driver's test over, have the permanent license in hand, and present the car title at the Department of Motor Vehicles office that had long lines and was located in the backside of an old mall several miles away.

When I presented my documents to the clerk, she said, "I cannot accept this because the title is in your and your husband's name." I told her my husband was deceased and pulled his death certificate from a sheaf of papers in my purse. She quickly replied, "Let me get my manager," and scurried away. The manager instructed me to get a copy of a particular form from the county in Texas where the will had been probated. I left choking back tears and second-guessing myself for having moved—probably too much change too quickly.

As I started reading the scene found in today's scripture, I drifted into imaginative prayer—a method of reading scripture using our imagination—which has been a treasured tradition in prayer for centuries. Saint Francis of Assisi used this method to encourage people to create nativity scenes at Christmas, a way to imagine the Holy Family as real people. Centuries later, Saint Ignatius of Loyola used this technique as well. Today I opened my imagination to enter the story of a bumpy boat ride.

After feeding the five thousand, Jesus makes his disciples get into a boat and go to the other side of the Galilean Sea while he goes up on a mountain to pray. Evening comes, and Jesus sees they are having a difficult time rowing against strong winds. He begins walking toward them on the sea. Thinking he is an apparition, they are terrified. But immediately Jesus speaks: "Take heart, it is I; do not be afraid." He joins them in the boat, and the strong winds cease.

I imagined myself in the boat, wind stinging my face, salt spray burning my eyes, hair whipping about my cheeks. Learning to be a widow is a bumpy, terrifying boat ride. Some days the pitching and tossing of my little vessel makes my head hurt, my stomach roil, my heart pound. Just when I think I can't continue, Jesus walks across the angry waves and climbs in my boat with me. I receive courage, comfort, strength from my Savior and Best Friend. Life goes forward. Seas calm and sunsets amaze. And like the disciples in this story, I am utterly astounded.

PRAYER: *Lord of sea and sky, you hear your people cry, and you come to give your life that they may be saved. O Lord, how incredibly mysterious and magnificent is your love. Amen.*

THOUGHT FOR THE DAY: God comes when God hears God's people cry.

WAIT, WAIT

READ PSALM 27:13-14; 46:10-11.

Wait for the LORD;
be strong and take heart
and wait for the LORD.

PSALM 27:14, NIV

Decades ago I attended support group meetings for newly single adults struggling with feelings of loss and grief that come with death and divorce. The reason I was hurting at that time in my life was divorce after a twenty-seven year marriage. Now I'm feeling the nauseating pain of grieving the death of my second husband, the true love of my life of seventeen years. The thought hit me today that some of those same stages of grief and agonizing times of aloneness have returned. One night the leader cautioned us, "Be careful. You are vulnerable now. I advise you not to rush into new relationships to fill the void in your lives. You must learn to live with the emptiness. Wait, wait." I have read the advice of many health professionals who suggest the wait should last a minimum of two years. However, they also note that no two people handle the journey in the same way and there is no locked-in one way to live our lives.

This morning I have no expectations of having another man in my life nor does this septuagenarian want a repeat experience of a spouse's long illness and years of exhaustive caregiving. Six months of heavy grief and transition have passed slowly. I'm still tired. What I am learning is there is no quick fix for solving the problem of grief for most of us. Some widows are working at a job, raising children, caring for elderly parents, and so on, and they are forced to continue active lives after their spouse dies. Others have to deal with financial and health problems that compound grief and loneliness. No matter our circumstances, the journey is difficult.

I bumped up against the "Wait, Wait" advice again today in my scripture reading: "Wait for the LORD; be strong and take heart." Waiting is not easy, especially for organized, efficient types. We have been hit by the crisis of losing our helpmate, which brings with it a spiritual crisis. Some days God seems far away, too remote to hear my soul's sighs. Yet when I practice time apart to wait, watch, and listen, God becomes present and renews my spirit. I don't know how this happens, but I know with certainty that my time apart with the Lord transforms and calms me mentally, physically, and spiritually. In the quiet, love is spoken. Love blesses; love heals.

Sitting alone late last night, I entered a spirit-conversation with my Lord. As I sat there perfectly still in body and mind—not praying, not talking, not thinking, not moving—I felt a soothing calm come over me. It was like I had found a gold mine of peace deep within. In the quiet, love was spoken again and again until my grief was temporarily lifted. I had the strange sensation that I was learning to befriend the emptiness. "Wait on the LORD; be of good courage, and He shall strengthen your heart" (Ps. 27:14, NKJV).

PRAYER: *Caring and compassionate God, you bless me with your presence and your peace. I come with a thankful heart to rest in the wonder of your love. Amen.*

THOUGHT FOR THE DAY: In the quiet, God's love speaks to us.

IN THE WILDERNESS

Then Jesus was led up by the Spirit into the wilderness to be tempted by the devil. . . . Then the devil left him, and suddenly angels came and waited on him.

MATTHEW 4:1, 11

When I left Texas after Bob's death to be near relatives in North Carolina, one of the losses was monthly sessions with my spiritual director, the Right Reverend Sam Hulsey. His friendship with Bob and me was a gift over many years. He gave me a reference and insisted I contact his good friend Reverend Stuart Hoke soon after the move. Monthly sessions with Reverend Hoke over the past fourteen months have made it clear I have received another gift. Sam helped me through my first six months of heavy grief, and Stuart picked up as I entered my next six months of tough but softer grieving.

Stuart often starts with this phrase: "Tell me what God is doing in your life." For the first four meetings, my response was the same: "I feel like God has led me into the wilderness. The outer life seems okay, but on the inside I'm struggling." When I tried to describe the wilderness, I thought about Jesus' baptism by John in the Jordan, when he was identified as the Chosen One, God's beloved Son, Messiah, and Savior. Immediately thereafter Jesus, led by the Spirit, went into the wilderness to be alone for forty days before embarking on his ministry.

Some scholars believe that the desert where Jesus went to be alone is called *Jeshimon*, meaning "devastation." It is an area between Jerusalem and the Dead Sea—a central plateau composed of rocks, jagged limestone, and dust heaps. At one side, the plateau drops one thousand two hundred feet through crags and precipices to the Dead Sea. Jesus—alone, hungry, tired, and vulnerable—was tested there.

A WIDOW'S PRAYER

63

Many times during previous months I felt dry, craggy, barren, vulnerable, and alone in my widowhood. The wilderness is not a place I wanted to go, but it seems all of us go there at some time. The death of a loved one, the loss of a job, a health crisis, the death of a dream, a major disappointment may catapult us into a place of agonizing introspection but also an experience of discovery. The question I faced was not if I would go into this wilderness but when and where I would go *from* it. I couldn't find a new church home. I didn't have my friends and old support system. How would I compensate for these critical losses? Who am I now that I am no longer someone's wife and caregiver? Where and how can I serve the Lord I love with all my heart in this new place? What is my value? My purpose?

Sam and Stuart have always encouraged the cultivation of the inner life: becoming ourselves as fully as we are able, seeking the riches of the soul's journey even in times of painful wilderness. I am slowly learning the lesson that self-discovery is potentially healing and holy.

PRAYER: *Eternal and everlasting Father, you have brought me into a time of grief and vulnerability. May my soul's odyssey bring me home to you where I find love, security, purpose, and value as your cherished child. Amen.*

THOUGHT FOR THE DAY: Our souls are restless until they find their haven in God.

TO THE MOON

READ PSALM 100.

Know that the LORD is God.
It is he that made us, and we are his;
we are his people, and the sheep of his pasture.

PSALM 100:3

A wise owl in the woods seen during a twilight walk triggered a reflective meditation the next morning. I thought about my husband's wisdom and concern his last month on this earth about how I would handle his death. Our pastor repeatedly reassured him I would be all right. "The Lord will take care of Nell. She's got me, her family, her church, and lots of friends to make sure she's okay. Not to worry." The pastor was right. I have struggled with grief and deep sadness, but I am learning to befriend life without my beloved. And to punctuate the affirmation that life does goes on, I like to imagine that Bob's spirit sometimes resides in an owl in the woods behind my new home.

While thumbing through a catalog one evening, I found a picture of a cute little owl sitting on a tree limb with a large full moon in the sky behind him. The message read: "I love you to the moon and back." Yes, I ordered it and hung it on the wall near a picture of my husband. It never fails to evoke a smile and a gladdened heart.

I am aware that traditionally the owl is known as the announcer of death. I recall a book I reviewed for a weekly newspaper column when I was a librarian back in the '70s. Margaret Craven is the author of the powerful, memorable classic *I Heard the Owl Call My Name*, a parable about the reconciliation of two cultures and two faiths, about life and death and the transforming power of love.

The book opens with the doctor telling the bishop that his young vicar, Mark Brian, has a terminal illness. The doctor and the bishop decide not to tell him. Instead Mark is sent to a remote area of the

Pacific Northwest to the ancient village of Kingcome to live among the natives where only the fundamentals count, where hunting and fishing remain a primary food source, and where manual labor is key to survival. Mark discovers the little church and vicarage are in terrible disrepair as he begins a journey of discovery that teaches him enough during his brief tour of duty there about the meaning of life to be ready to die.

On his first Christmas Eve, Mark stands waiting in hushed silence next to a statue of Jesus holding a little lamb. Candlelight shines on the sad eyes. Sorrow and loneliness dwell in this remote community. But then Mark opens the church doors and sees the villagers coming with their flickering lanterns, single file along the path to the church. "For the first time he knew them for what they were, the people of his hand and the sheep of his pasture, and he knew how deep was his commitment to them."*

As time goes on, the vicar does hear the owl call his name. He grows weak, and the bishop decides to send a replacement. Mark wonders how he will live back in the old world. He, like the salmon, comes up the river to give his life. He "had made friends with loneliness, with death and deprivation." Yet when his back is against the wall, his faith remains strong and solid.

Sometimes we are sad and lonely, but like Mark, we know Christ is greater than our most debilitating sorrow. Our God loves us to the moon and back.

PRAYER: *Thank You, Good Shepherd, for loving your people—the sheep of your pasture. I am grateful I can trust you to be present in all circumstances of my life. Amen.*

THOUGHT FOR THE DAY: Christ is greater than our most debilitating sorrow.

*Margaret Craven, *I Heard the Owl Call My Name* (New York: Dell Publishing, 1973), 58, 145.

NOT GUILTY

READ EPHESIANS 2:4-9.

But God, who is rich in mercy, out of the great love with which he loved us even when we were dead through our trespasses, made us alive together with Christ—by grace you have been saved.

EPHESIANS 2:4-5

The attractive older woman sat quietly in the pew in front of me. When the service ended, I introduced myself. In a matter of minutes I learned the commonality of our life stories. We both were struggling with the newness and shock of widowhood (she for eight months and fifteen months for me). I asked if her husband had been sick for a long time.

Softly she began to tell me how her husband of fifty plus years had fallen, hit his head, and developed blood clots in his brain. He entered his eternal rest within two months. She told me how she left his hospital room only briefly during those weeks because the two of them had promised one another to be present when death came. One day she went home briefly to shower and eat, and, to her bewilderment, he died before she returned.

"I feel so bad; I didn't keep my promise. I was only gone a short time," she said in a whisper while choking back tears.

I told her I understood because I was not in the room when Bob took his last breath. I had gone to get a cup of coffee. But he had not made me promise I would be there. I tend to think, even in his coma, he planned for me to be out of the room. He always said he couldn't stand to see me cry. It tore him up when I was sad and weepy. Yes, I cried, but, at the same time, I was immensely relieved his suffering was over.

I have played that game of regret that I did not do some things differently. Many of us widows have a hard time with unwarranted guilt. We magically think we could have somehow, some way done more. Not only are we burdened with the physical, emotional, and mental demands of dealing with the loss of our loved ones and all that entails, but also we add on unmerited, irrational burdens of guilt because we didn't do everything perfectly.

I've experienced a shift in thinking about the past. It would be prideful to think I could have been the perfect wife, caregiver, lover, best friend. I can't even be the perfect widow. Thanks be to God, I don't have to be perfect at being anyone or anything. I can only be a child of God, loved and forgiven, saved by grace, hugged and cherished today and into eternity. I know a hardworking, single woman who loves the Lord and always exudes joy and kindness no matter her circumstances. When asked, "How are you?" she responds, "I am blessed and highly favored." She gets it right. And the good news is we too are blessed and highly favored.

PRAYER: *Merciful Lord, I am grateful that out of your great love and mercy, you have saved me and raised me up through the immeasurable riches of your grace in kindness towards me in Christ Jesus. Amen.*

THOUGHT FOR THE DAY: The riches of God's grace are immeasurable.

ETTY

READ HABAKKUK 3:17-19.

Though the fig tree does not blossom,
and no fruit is on the vines; . . .
and there is no herd in the stalls,
yet I will rejoice in the LORD;
I will exult in the God of my salvation.

HABAKKUK 3:17-18

The prophet Habakkuk's reports make current conditions look bleak; he has no crops or animals that are needed for survival. God's saving acts are not yet evident; the people and the land continue to suffer. But Habakkuk holds on to his vision and his trust in God's saving power. He holds on to his faith, and his faith directs him to rejoice and praise God regardless of his difficult circumstances.

Recently I have learned about a young Jewish woman named Etty (Esther) Hillesum who was born in 1914 in the Netherlands. She lived in Middelburg with her parents and her two brothers and later lived in Amsterdam during the Nazi occupation. She received her master's in Dutch law, worked as a teacher, and moved in anti-fascist student circles. Upon recommendation of her therapist, Julius Spier, she began keeping diaries to help with her depression. Her letters and *An Interrupted Life: The Diaries of Etty Hillesum 1941–43* reveal the deep spiritual life of a thinker and a mystic. In spite of her restless, disrupted, difficult circumstances, she was able to find God and be transformed by faith. She became a woman full of love and inner peace and declared she lived in constant intimacy with God.

In the summer of 1942, Etty volunteered to go with the first group of Jews being deported from Amsterdam to a nearby detention camp. It was there that she received news that her therapist, mentor, friend, and lover, Spier had died. She saw this loss in the context of the larger affliction facing the Jewish people and wrote, "To think that one small human heart can experience so much, oh God, so much suffering and so much love, I am so grateful to You, God, for having chosen my heart, in these times, to experience all the things it has experienced."*

Etty was deported and eventually executed in Gross-Rosen concentration camp in Auschwitz, Poland, in 1943 at the age of twenty-nine. Before her departure, she gave the diaries to a friend, and they were later translated and published in 1984 by Random House. Her life story has been made into a one-woman theatrical play by Susan Stein, and it is playing around the country to rave reviews.

The kind of faith that lives with the comingling of evil and death, difficulty and hardship, but holds on to hope and gratitude to God is rare and inspirational. Etty's experience—like that of Habakkuk's vision—shows that even when everything looks hopeless, God is a God of salvation. God is with Habakkuk, Etty, us.

Remember as children how we spun around in circles until we felt dizzy and disoriented? This first year of widowhood feels like that. Etty thanked God for choosing her heart to experience so much love and so much suffering. My hope is to someday have her inner peace and her grateful openness for whatever life brings.

PRAYER: *Father God, my life is filled with good and beautiful, difficult and afflicting experiences. Transform and reorient me to a place of hope and trust in the reality that you are not beyond me but with me in the midst of everyday life. Amen.*

THOUGHT FOR THE DAY: In well-being and in woe, God is always with us.

*I was first introduced to Etty Hillesum in an article by Mark S. Burrows and John H. Ohlson, Jr. titled "Love Is a Direction" that appeared in *Weavings* 27, no. 4 (Aug/Sept/Oct 2012): 14–15. Etty Hillesum, *An Interrupted Life: The Diaries, 1941–193*, and *Letters from Westerbork*, trans. Arnold J. Pomerans (New York: Henry Holt, 1996), 198.

HASSLED AT THE DMV

READ PSALM 46:10 AND NUMBERS 6:24-26.

"The LORD make his face shine on you
and be gracious to you;
the LORD turn his face toward you
and give you peace."

NUMBERS 6:25-26, NIV

Yesterday was beyond difficult; I experienced the ultimate frustration and anxiety. I wanted to return to my old life. I felt like a victim, like someone totally helpless to change an out-of-control, downwardly spiraling destiny. Sounds a bit melodramatic now, but that's how I felt.

My mission was to get the new car tag before my sixty-five days in this new state ran out. Finding the Department of Motor Vehicles office, located in the remote corner of a mall across town, on my first visit had been a feat. The line winding out the big glass door had tipped me off. But this was my fourth time to come. The first trip I was told by a snippy little clerk that I would have to come back when I had my permanent state driver's license—the temporary one was unacceptable.

When the permanent license came, I returned only to be told by another snippy clerk that I had to bring my car title. I drove home and got the title out of the safe. On the third trip I was told the title was unacceptable because it had both my husband's name and mine on it. When I produced a death certificate, the clerk said, "I have to get my supervisor." It was a long wait before the supervisor came to inform me that I would need to produce letters of testamentary from Tarrant County, Texas.

Back home, I found the phone number on the Internet and called. I was told North Carolina was wrong and to take to the DMV the certified copy of "the order admitting will to probate as a muniment of title." I found said document, went back, and stood in line. I explained to the clerk I was there to get my North Carolina car tag and handed her my stack of papers. She took a quick look and said, "I have to get my supervisor." After some minutes, the clerk returned and handed me my car tag. But she did not give the title back to me. I asked for it and was told they would issue a new one without my husband's name on it. I didn't understand why I couldn't hang on to it until the new one came in two weeks. "You can't," the woman snapped and hurriedly walked away. This whole DMV experience profoundly deepened my sense of loss and vulnerability. I sat in the car and cried.

Following a restless night, I ate a bowl of oatmeal and went to my "prayer chair." I lit the candle and wearily began to read scripture and daily devotions. In *Jesus Calling: Enjoying Peace in His Presence* by Sarah Young, I found these words:

"Take time to *be still* in My Presence. The more hassled you feel, the more you need this sacred space of communion with Me. Breathe slowly and deeply. Relax in My holy Presence while *My Face shines upon you.* This is how you receive My Peace."*

The anxious stomach knots, the painful tension in neck and shoulder muscles, and the stress headache slowly eased their grip on my body and heart. "The Lord turn his face toward you and give you his peace." With this message, I could journey forward.

PRAYER: *Thank you, Lord, for coming to me with words of encouragement. Amen.*

THOUGHT FOR THE DAY: God walks with us through all our trials and brings peace.

*Sarah Young, *Jesus Calling: Enjoying Peace in His Presence* (Nashville, TN: Thomas Nelson, 2004), 300.

VALENTINE'S DAY

READ EPHESIANS 3:16-19.

---

*I pray that you may have the power to comprehend, with all
the saints, what is the breadth and length and height and
depth, and to know the love of Christ that surpasses knowledge, so that you may be filled with all the fullness of God.*

EPHESIANS 3:18-19

Although there are many legends and traditions associated with
Saint Valentine and his special day, I like a popular tradition that
identifies Saint Valentine as a former bishop of Terni, a city in central
Italy. While under arrest for marrying Christian couples, he discussed
his faith and the validity of Jesus with his jailer Asterius. The jailer
decided to put Valentine to the test and brought his blind daughter
to him. A deal was made that if the child's sight was restored, Asterius
was to destroy all household gods, fast for three days, and then be
baptized. When the girl was healed, the jailer obeyed. His family and
forty others were baptized, and Asterius freed all Christian inmates
under his authority.

Valentine was arrested again for refusing to worship pagan gods.
When he tried to convince Emperor Claudius II to embrace Christi-
anity, the emperor condemned Valentine to be beaten and beheaded.
Legend has it that on the day of his execution—February 14—he left
the jailer's daughter a note signed, "Your Valentine."

This is my first Valentine's Day without my sweetheart, a day usually celebrated with flowers, chocolates, letters, cards, or gifts expressing romance and devotion. I have such a hole in my heart now that he
is gone. I hurt. My husband's absence is strongly present today, but I
go on, with comfort from the Lord, all the while a bit brokenhearted.

My first year as a widow has turned out to be a season of wilderness, bewilderment, and vulnerability. I feel God is emptying me,

taking everything away, including my ambition to serve, to minister, to do anything at all. I feel stripped down, possessing nothing, cracked open without expectations. Sitting in a comfy chair wrapped in a woolen afghan, watching big, wet snowflakes out the window, I wait. I wait for something, even if there will be nothing to fill the void in my broken heart today. Deep, heavy sorrow evokes the idea that the capacity to love carries with it the potential for suffering.

I think about Saint Valentine and his love for Jesus that helped him heal a blind child and risk his neck for the Great Commission's call to teach, share God's love story, and baptize. Jesus so radically loved, suffered, and redeemed that the mystery of God's heart was exposed and offered to each of us. I hope that somehow God can find a way to use my suffering and my grief to open the doorway of my heart so that I may experience loving God and neighbor more deeply. I don't want to deny my pain or imagine I can be exempt from grief. Numbing my heart could be tragic too. Perhaps with God's help I can shift my focus from my sorrowing self and answer the invitation to be a valentine to someone who needs a little red heart today.

PRAYER: *O love of Christ that fills me with the fullness of God and heals my broken heart, use my experience of profound sorrow to teach me to be more loving. Amen.*

THOUGHT FOR THE DAY: Through Christ, we can learn to love even in the midst of sorrow.

ARE WE THERE YET?

READ JOSHUA 1:1-6, 9.

---

*"I hereby command you: Be strong and courageous;
do not be frightened or dismayed, for the LORD your God is
with you wherever you go."*

JOSHUA 1:9

The workshop leader gave us instructions: "You have seven minutes to make a time line of your life." I quickly turned my sheet of paper sideways and drew a horizontal line from left to right and began labeling sections—childhood, high school, college, first job, marriage, arrival of children, and so on. A neat, orderly progression. At the end of the exercise, the leader rose, went to the newsprint easel, and began drawing a line that looped, squiggled, zigzagged, ran up and down, back and forth. He told us his life had been chaotic, similar to that of the Israelites wandering in the desert for forty years while they mumbled about Egyptian melons, leeks, cucumbers, and the good ol' days. Thirty-five years have passed since that workshop, and I know now the leader was absolutely on point about the way life is—often messy, unpredictable, and loopy. Moses did not get to enter the Promised Land; the Messiah rode a donkey and was crucified. One surprise after another.

On many occasions I have thought of my journey in grief to be like a disorienting experience in the desert. I have zigzagged through a year of "firsts": first Father's Day, first birthday, first Thanksgiving, first Christmas, first anniversary, first Valentine's Day, and other special events that threw me into thinking about my beloved and his death. They say the second year is better for most people. In the third year many experience greater acceptance of the fact that although life will never be the same, it can be good again. But not always. I know a widow who cries easily when she talks about her husband decades after his death. Another was a recluse for six years. Grief is personal; no two of us are going to do it alike.

During a six-week seminar offered by my hospice grief counselor, I remember her repeating many times that grief is a slow and painful process that cannot be hurried. We cannot go around it, although many try with all sorts of "painkillers." We must go through it; there are no shortcuts. The pace may depend on whether the loved one died suddenly or suffered a long illness. A woman I know accepted her husband's death but to this day cannot resolve the grief associated with her daughter's murder. Grief is so subjective.

Our culture permits the bereaved to be sad at the funeral, but in a few weeks or months, unfortunately, many family and friends want us to hurry up and get over our grief and depression. But it is during the desert of our grief that we need to surrender to the natural process of healing that will lead to a place of resolve, renewal, and peace. We go to the desert and experience the pain as it needs to be. Rather than running from it, I am finding I need a space each day to go to the desert, acknowledge my feelings, and reflect on my loss. Then I can go forward for a while before I need to retreat again.

Are we there yet? Is the end of this journey in grief drawing near? No, not yet. Perhaps there will always be a hole in my heart. In the meantime I am holding on to the Lord's words to Joshua and the Israelites to be strong and courageous "for the LORD your God is with you wherever you go." We walk the hard road together.

PRAYER: *Help me, Lord God, to find solace in your promise always to be with me. Amen.*

THOUGHT FOR THE DAY: God walks with us through all hardships and transitions.

SPRING THAW

READ ISAIAH 35:1-2.

The wilderness and the dry land shall be glad,
the desert shall rejoice and blossom;
like the crocus it shall blossom abundantly,
and rejoice with joy and singing.

ISAIAH 35:1-2

The winter has been cold, rainy, gray, dismal, icy. Today I feel chilled and frozen in my grief. Lent has begun—that period in the church year when we enter a time of self-examination and penitence, a period of forty days modeled after the forty days Jesus spent in the desert following his baptism. I find myself being tested in the wilderness, but I feel stuck here indefinitely. It has been almost a year since Bob died, and I expected to be happier by now. I struggle with much change, much grief.

This morning I found a quote I had written in my journal from a Lenten booklet of meditations by members of Trinity Episcopal Church, Fort Worth, Texas. It came from a devotion by Celia Ledbetter, and I remain haunted by her words: "We know who we are and where we are going. Until . . . a death, a disease, an injustice occurs and our confident tidy little basis of life is challenged. Of course we pray, we're Christians! But what happens when nothing happens?"

I do believe in the recesses of my soul that my grief will soften, thaw, someday, but right now I struggle with huge transitions of moving to a new home in a new state while trudging through a sluggish sadness. I feel out of place, a stranger, a "wandering Aramean" (see Deuteronomy 26:5) who is on the journey and homesick. As I plod along in wet, cold interior and exterior environments, my slippery steps reverberate with a steady drone of "Wait, wait, wait." I feel like a big, ugly, brown, lifeless daffodil bulb buried deep beneath the ice. The prophet Isaiah reminds me that God is doing new things even while I walk in the wilderness: "the dry land shall be glad" and the crocus "shall blossom abundantly." But today it feels like nothing is happening; hope is hanging by a fragile thread. What happens when nothing happens? We simply wait.

Grieving is a tough process and what the counselor told me seems to be true: "The first year is the hardest for most people, and then it becomes less intense." And so my mantra is this: *Wait, wait, wait on the Lord—for as long as it takes.* My parched lips and dry mouth yearn for quenching water, and yet the sandy desert yields nothing more than a trickle of tears. I read Isaiah and hope for transformation. I tell myself, *Nell, allow the teardrops to sustain you until a spring thaw arrives and ushers in a time of overflowing love and joy again. Hang on. God's promises are true in God's own time. So stop whining; count blessings. Trust that the grief will thaw, and soon the hillside will be covered with golden daffodils dancing in the spring breeze.*

PRAYER: *God of hope and mercy, God of seasons of joy and sadness, help me to hold on to your promise that a time of rejoicing is coming—even while I must wait and struggle with deep grief and frozen spirit. Amen.*

THOUGHT FOR THE DAY: God's promises are true in God's own time.

HEALING
AND
HOPE

I pray that the God of our Lord Jesus Christ, the Father of glory, may give you a spirit of wisdom and revelation as you come to know him, so that, with the eyes of your heart enlightened, you may know what is the hope to which he has called you.

EPHESIANS 1:17-18

#1 TEACHER

READ MATTHEW 5:1-10.

*Now when Jesus saw the crowds, he went up on a
mountainside and sat down. His disciples came to him,
and he began to teach them.*

MATTHEW 5:1-2, NIV

About fifteen months after Bob's death, I realized I was engaged
in a kind of identity crisis because I was no longer a wife and caregiver. My children were grown, my grandkids were growing up and
some getting married, my mother was safely and happily settled in
assisted living, and my responsibilities (except to myself) had mostly
disappeared. I moved to a new city and state to be near family and
settled in a condo in the woods. I had been busy during the second
six months after Bob died with moving, sewing curtains and pillows,
decorating, and immersing myself in a "nesting phase" of building a
new home for me and dog Molly.

But after that "nesting phase," I wrestled anew with my identity.
I thought about who I was before I was wife, mother, grandmother,
librarian, and church educator. What kind of dreams did I have?
Where had I found my "bliss"? What had I wanted to do with the
rest of my life? I talked with another widow about this over supper
one night. She worked a full-time job but was taking a history course
because she always loved history. Another friend had taken up piano
lessons for the first time in her life.

One thing about my identity had become clear: I was a church-
woman in need of a church home. It took a while to discover a church
that "fit," but once I made the commitment, I jumped in fully. As a
former professional church educator, I knew volunteers are needed and
welcomed. I responded to the call to join the Education Committee.

I find joy in teaching and learning, so I announced that I would be willing to teach or facilitate wherever there was a need. A few weeks later I received a call from the church office that a woman had inquired if there was someone who might come to her retirement community and offer a Bible study. Generally five people, all eager students, attend.

At the first gathering I asked what the group members wanted to study. One wanted the Gospels, another the Old Testament; others had no opinion. I suggested we study Matthew as a compromise since it qualifies as a Gospel while still containing over sixty quotations from the Old Testament. The book of Matthew is designed to teach the connections among the Hebrew scriptures, prophecies, and Jesus, the Messiah. The choice seems to have been inspired, and the students have been faithful in preparation and serious study. Matthew has been tagged "The Teacher's Gospel" because the Gospel is comprised of five organized discourses of Jesus' teachings. As I prepared to lead, I sensed an invitation to dig deeper into my faith. I had found my bliss.

The students thank me profusely after each session. Last night I was deeply touched by a Valentine gift from two members: a box labeled #1 Teacher containing a hollow milk chocolate apple wrapped in red foil with a green foil leaf attached. I feel as though I'm making a difference in their lives while living into who I am meant to be.

PRAYER: *Thank you, Jesus, Messiah, Teacher, for connections I am making with others and with you through the power of Bible study. Amen.*

THOUGHT FOR THE DAY: How are we being invited to dig deeper in our faith?

BRRRRR BLUES

READ JOHN 15:9-11.

"As the Father has loved me, so I have loved you;
abide in my love."

JOHN 15:9

Brrrr, brrr, brrr—it's bitterly cold. The winter storm came in suddenly yesterday and within three hours, there were six inches of white, powdery snow covering everything. A state of emergency was declared. Conditions were so dangerous that the Duke versus Carolina men's basketball game had to be rescheduled because the buses could not get out. That's cold! Everyone has been advised to stay home again today, and the second wave of snow, sleet, and ice began about an hour ago. Thank goodness I still have power, but with more ice accumulating on the trees, my good fortune could change. Loss of power will mean loss of heat. That would bring a double dose of the "Brrrr Blues."

This winter has been exceptionally cold with one wave of winter storm after another in many sections of the country. Temperatures have been below freezing; sunshine has been rare. I normally have to fight the blues each January, but this winter has extended that challenge into February. Lack of sunshine, cabin fever, little opportunity for socialization, cold hands and nose, bulky clothing—such issues have fostered a disquieted spirit that longs for a fireside chat over a cup of hot chocolate with my late husband. But that is not to be.

Last night I wrapped up in a quilt and finished reading an insightful book by William Bridges titled *Transitions: Making Sense of Life's Changes.* Bridges discusses the inevitability of change and offers strategies for understanding the difficult and confusing times in our lives. According to Bridges, transitions have three sections: endings, neutral zones, and new beginnings. I feel like I have been through most of the endings phase of saying good-bye to my husband, my old identity as wife and caregiver, my former home with him in Texas, our church family, our neighbors, my life as I had known it. This morning as I sit (still wrapped up in a quilt) looking out at the winter wonderland (sans sunshine to make it glisten), it occurs to me that I am in that "neutral zone" Bridges describes as the second hurdle of transition, a seemingly unproductive time-out when I feel disconnected from the past and emotionally unconnected to the present. He describes his experience of the stage this way: "I had shed the shell of my old identity like a lobster, and I was staying close to the rocks because I was still soft and vulnerable. I'd have a new and better-fitting identity in time, but for now I'd have to go a little slowly."*

Winter is fallow time when all seems asleep, still, lifeless, slow. That is where I find myself today. And yet I recall the words Jesus spoke to his disciples during their last meal together: "Abide in my love." This phrase means more than simple perseverance. I hold on to God's hand and trust that the silence, the fallow time, the stillness are working toward a reorientation of loving service in God's world. As I surrender to the "Brrrrr Blues," I find myself feeling "soft and vulnerable." Still, I abide, and I wait.

PRAYER: *God of ever-present help in time of transition and change, come sit with me and whisper in my ear words of comforting love that will warm my heart and mind in the wintertime of my life. Amen.*

THOUGHT FOR THE DAY: No matter the season, we can find comfort in God's love.

---

*William Bridges, *Transitions: Making Sense of Life's Changes*, 2nd ed. (Cambridge, MA: Da Capo Press/Perseus Books, 2004), 117.

HOLD ON TO THE PLOW

READ 2 TIMOTHY 3:10-17.

All Scripture is God-breathed and is useful for teaching,
rebuking, correcting and training in righteousness.

2 TIMOTHY 3:16, NIV

Keep your hand on the plow, hold on, hold on.
Nora said you done lost track,
You can't plow straight and keep a-looking back.

If you wanna get to heaven let me tell you how,
Just keep your hand on the gospel plow.
. . .
Hold on! Oh, Brother, hold on!
Hold on! Oh, Sister, hold on!

—Traditional Spiritual

Rich harmonies of eighty choral voices filled the vaulted chapel with soulful sounds and rocking rhythms of an old spiritual. Worshipers began to sway; smiles appeared on faces. The congregation came alive—lost in wonder, love, and praise—in the presence of the Lord.

Later that afternoon, I thought about the words of the offertory message ("Just keep your hand on the gospel plow") as I began to prepare for a midweek Bible study. I am truly sustained by daily scriptures and meditations. Time in my little "prayer chair" turns my heart and mind toward my Maker and Redeemer every morning. I don't think I could have made it through a single day without that discipline, and I certainly would not have made it through the days of heavy grief in recent years. Even during those difficult months when I knew my husband's health was failing, I would return to my Bible and prayers to be reminded of the good news that we are God's beloved and God has a plan of extravagant, saving grace. I held on to the plow—even when dubious and uncertain of its efficacy.

Bible study with a group of seekers has always been a favorite activity of mine. When Bob's health made a serious decline the last months of his life, I dropped out of my study group. I didn't want to leave him alone for one single evening. I also was exhausted simply trying to get through the day. A year after his death, it dawned on me one of the missing components for moving on with my life in my new location was a group study. I tried several until I learned that the church I was visiting had a Bible study using the exact same book I was using when I had dropped out of my study group eighteen months earlier. No longer looking back, I took hold of that gospel plow with new Christian brothers and sisters who were holding on to their plows. My grief softened immediately.

We need community—especially in times of unwanted crisis. We need the God-breathed Word, the scriptures. As we read, study, store God's Word in our hearts, and use it to guide our footsteps, the Word becomes the voice that speaks of God's steadfast love and mercy. I now facilitate a Bible group and each session begins with lighting a white candle while I say, "Thy word is a lamp unto [our] feet, and a light unto [our] path" (Ps. 119:105, KJV). Then together we say, "The Light of Christ has come into the world." We open our Bibles and take hold of the good news plow.

PRAYER: *Almighty God, as you inspire me through scripture, teach me to follow you with a loving heart and obedient will. May I plow straight into the Promised Land with my community of Christian brothers and sisters, all to the glory of your name. Amen.*

THOUGHT FOR THE DAY: Scripture teaches us that we are beloved children of God.

LUKE

Read Psalm 89:1-4.

I will sing of your steadfast love, O Lord, forever;
with my mouth I will proclaim your faithfulness to all
generations.

Psalm 89:1

My husband was elated with the news that Ellen, a granddaughter, and her husband were expecting a baby. He thanked God for the privilege of being a great-grandfather. But then his health went into sharp decline, he entered hospice care, and shortly thereafter he died. He would not get to hold the firstborn of the new generation.

Soon after Bob's memorial service, Ellen had a miscarriage, and my family's grief was compounded. Prayers began in earnest for healing and for another baby. No one mentioned the situation, but we all knew it was tugging at our hearts. And then the wonderful news came of another pregnancy. I prayed fervently every morning, and my stepdaughter (and grandmother-to-be) continued to report all was going well.

Excitedly I made the trip with other family members to Texas for Ellen's baby shower. Such a joyous reunion we had. Hope and glad hearts overflowed into every corner of space surrounding the soon-to-be parents, family, and friends. Gifts were generous and thoughtful, each one expressing love and affection. Three generations gathered together to joyfully support and prepare for the arrival of the fourth.

Luke arrived the morning of September 14, 2013—a healthy, little boy. The delivery went well. I am now a great-grandmother, and my fond hope is that somehow Bob knows about the little guy and that our prayers have been answered.

Luke's arrival sent me to my journal to express joy and also my regret that Bob would never hold this child. Then I began to think about the gift Luke would be to the world and how we are gifts for one another. I thought about the innocence of a child and how life can batter our hearts and courage. I pray for little Luke. I pray for myself and for others suffering with grief. May we nourish the children within us. May we birth a wisdom molded out of our grieving. May we ask for newness in our solitary lives so that we can boldly offer ourselves as gifts and blessings to the world. And together let us sing a song of the Lord's faithfulness to all generations this day and always.

PRAYER: *Steadfast and compassionate God and Father of all, show me this day a way to express love, encouragement, and affirmation to someone who needs the gift of hope. Amen.*

THOUGHT FOR THE DAY: We thank God for children and the hope they bring to the world.

THE DOGWOOD TREE

READ MARK 15:16-20.

*And [the soldiers] clothed [Jesus] in a purple cloak; and
after twisting some thorns into a crown, they put it on him.*

MARK 15:17

The woods near my childhood home in Mississippi provided a wondrous playground among tall, stately, loblolly pines and shorter, deciduous dogwoods. I was especially fascinated by the seasonal changes of the dogwoods—flowering in spring, leaves turning red in autumn, and the appearance of clusters of shiny, ruby red, ovoid berries in winter. This was truly miraculous to my inquiring child-spirit.

That feeling of wonder returned when I took a walk in the woods near my North Carolina home. Nestled among towering pines, I spotted a small, bare dogwood with bright red berry bunches. "The Legend of the Dogwood Tree," learned in Miss Olsen's third-grade Sunday school class, popped into my mind as I strolled around the bend toward my condo.

The Bible does not tell us what type of wood was used for the cross Jesus was crucified on, and Roman history does not go into specifics about cross construction. But the legend claims that in Jesus' time, the dogwood grew to the size of oak and other forest trees. Because its wood was so strong, its timber was chosen for the cross of Jesus. The tree agonized when it learned it was to be used for such a cruel purpose. Jesus felt the tree's sadness about his crucifixion and made a promise to the dogwood that from that day forward it's trunk and limbs would be bent and twisted and too small to produce a cross. Jesus decreed that dogwood blossoms would be in the form of a cross with two long and two short petals. The edge of each petal would show nail prints, brown with rust and stained with blood. The center of the flower would look like a crown of thorns; the berries would symbolize drops of blood shed for the redemption of the world.

I studied that little dogwood tree with its brown, scaly bark and peered closely at the berry clusters glistening in the sunshine. Memories of my husband's "crown of thorns"—a name we used for the hideous metal halo he wore three different times after neck surgeries—brought me to tears. Bob bore deep permanent scars from where the screws were drilled into his skull to hold that awful cage in place. One of my challenges was to cleanse the blood drops from around the screws. Time has not softened those memories.

Like the dogwood of legend, I felt such sadness and empathy for my husband with his chronic pain. He too was a man of sorrow and suffering. Both my Lord and Bob inspire me with the courage to persevere. And so I go forward from childhood to widowhood with an awareness of God's love being played out in the life cycles of a humble dogwood tree and within my own spirit's journey.

PRAYER: *Pain-Bearer, Lord of life and love, pour out on me an awareness of your presence in all aspects of my life each day. Thank you for the wonders of nature and the gifts of cherished relationships. Amen.*

THOUGHT FOR THE DAY: We see love's redeeming work in the Cross.

THE OWL

READ COLOSSIANS 2:2-5.

For though I am absent in body, yet I am with you in spirit.

COLOSSIANS 2:5

My rescue dog, Molly, and I moved to a condo in the North Carolina woods after Bob died. The walk at dusk became a favorite part of our routine and helped with the onslaught of grief that often struck at suppertime. Eating alone can make for a difficult transition.

On one of those walks a few months after we moved, I had the eerie sensation of being watched. I looked around. On a low tree limb only yards away sat a magnificent feathered creature with big yellow eyes in the middle of gold facial disks. We stared at each other in a kind of query that whispered, "Don't I know you from somewhere?" Molly tugged at her leash, and we strode on while those amazing eyes observed our every step.

As Molly and I passed the owl again on the way home, the owl repeated its silent watching. Barely audibly I spoke, "Mr. Noonan, is that you? Are you watching us? Are you guiding us from heaven with your wisdom and guarding us from harm in our new home? I hope so." A strange, tremendously comforting thought—my deceased husband present in my life somehow.

Two or three months will pass, and I won't see the owl. And then suddenly I will have that graced experience again when I see the owl watching Molly and me. Sometimes in the interim, I hear low, sonorous, far-carrying hoots, calling to a mate—to me perhaps.

These puzzling rendezvous set me on a search to know more about owls. I learned that in many dream interpretations across several cultures, the owl can represent a deceased family member and is often associated with departed souls. One traditional meaning of the owl is the announcement of death, not in a frightening way but as a symbol of a life transition. It could mean physical death or entering "new life." The owl also may offer the inspiration and guidance necessary to explore the unknown and the mystery of life.

Paul's letter to the church in Colossae contained the encouraging words that he was absent in body but not in spirit. Bob is no longer with me, and yet I sense our covenantal love at my core, pushing me forward. The owl in the woods also sustains and reminds me of God's presence always—watching, guiding, loving, surprising with a soft *hoo, hoo-hoo, hoo.*

PRAYER: *O Divine Spirit of Creation, Source of great learning and new discovery, teach me not to fear life transitions but to trust in your abounding love. May I therefore, with the gift of memory, walk through my days with gratitude for all the events of my life. Amen.*

THOUGHT FOR THE DAY: God always watches over us.

A TOUGH NUT

READ GENESIS 2:4-9.

Now the LORD God had planted a garden in the east, in Eden; and there he put the man he had formed. The LORD God made all kinds of trees grow out of the ground—trees that were pleasing to the eye and good for food.

GENESIS 2:8-9, NIV

I noticed something that looked like a little, earthy-brown dome atop a gray-green mossy patch next to the path where the dog and I were walking. Curious to know about this small thing (an inch or so in diameter), I bent down and picked it up. The surface was tough and heavily pocked. Then I turned it over and discovered the object was half of a nut, which I later identified as the fruit of a dark walnut tree. The inside of the cracked nut contained a light tan, heart-shaped piece. It was pierced with two oval holes that looked like eyes on a face.

Earlier that day I had been reading *The Unwanted Gift of Grief: A Ministry Approach* by Tim P. VanDuivendyk. My grief counselor gave me the book, and it has had a hugely helpful influence on my journey. VanDuivendyk states the following:

> When we lose someone to death, part of our identity is lost and must be reshaped over a long period of healing and transformation. We have to differentiate from that loved person and the life we had together in order to heal and go on with our lives. We do this by internalizing this person's love and taking that love with us as we recreate a new life.*

I knew that little nut was a reminder from a benevolent, gracious Creator that love—mine, Bob's, ours, God's—permeates everything that was, is, and will be. That moment was a gift from God.

Later as I reflected on the lesson of the little nut, I recalled readings from a fourteenth-century anchoress named Julian of Norwich. In the fifth chapter of *The Revelations of Divine Love,* she writes this:

Also in this revelation He showed a little thing,
    the size of an hazel nut
    in the palm of my hand,
    and it was as round as a ball.

I looked at it with the eye of my understanding and thought:
    "What can this be?"
And it was generally answered thus: "It is all that is made."

I marveled how it could continue,
    because it seemed to me it could suddenly have sunk
    into nothingness because of its littleness.
And I was answered in my understanding:
    "It continueth and always shall, because God loveth it;
    and in this way *everything* hath its being by the love of
    God."**

God must truly delight in surprises. Who else would send a love note in a tough, little nut?

PRAYER: *God of abundant gifts, open my eyes and heart to find the simple revelations of love you offer every day. Amen.*

THOUGHT FOR THE DAY: Open our eyes to see the simple gifts of God's love.

*Tim P. VanDuivendyk, *The Unwanted Gift of Grief: A Ministry Approach* (New York: Haworth Pastoral Press, 2006), 47.

**Father John-Julian, ed. and trans., *A Lesson of Love: the Revelations of Julian of Norwich* (New York: Walker and Company, 1988), 11–12.

THE RINGS

READ ROMANS 8:15-17 AND 1 PETER 3:4.

When we cry "Abba! Father!" it is that very Spirit bearing witness with our spirit that we are children of God.

ROMANS 8:15-16

Let your adornment be the inner self with the lasting beauty of a gentle and quiet spirit, which is very precious in God's sight.

1 PETER 3:4

As humans, we all struggle—regardless of age or stage, whether we are one or one hundred and one, whether we are married, single, divorced, or widowed—with two lifelong issues. The first one is identity—Who am I? What gives me value and worth?—and the other is purpose—Why am I here? What am I to do with my life? Life-changing events and experiences, such as caregiving and the loss of a loved one, collide with those issues in a cataclysmic way. I left my job and spent seven years taking care of my chronically ill husband. I identified as wife and caregiver. Caring for Bob became my work, my vocation, my purpose, my value—to be a devoted helpmate "until death do us part."

Several widow friends told me the first year of widowhood is the hardest, that the grief would ease up in later years, that joy would return. Now that I am seventeen months on the other side of Bob's death, I can say that has been true for me. I suppose there will always be a hole in my heart, and occasionally "little puddles of grief" will take me by surprise, but I do walk lighter. Some days I skip and hop and dance. I don't count losses. Following the advice of my ninety-five-year-old mother, a widow herself for many years, I count my blessings and have found them to be extravagantly abundant.

One of those blessings crept up on me and popped out in my journal this week. I realized I now have a freedom in my aloneness to be me. I am no longer someone's caregiver. I am no longer someone's wife. I can watch whatever I want on television and eat anything my taste buds crave. The laundry load and housework and doctor's visits have shrunk. The décor in my new home has a strong feminine flavor and no longer has to accommodate scooters and medical equipment. I have more time to reflect, to be silent, to pay attention to my inner self. I like it.

I've spoken with other widows about their decision of whether to continue wearing a wedding or engagement ring. Their answers varied. Some put them away and did not wear them after their husbands' deaths. Others put them on a chain and wore them as a necklace. Some decided to wear them for the rest of their lives, and others chose to wear them on their right hand. I struggled with what to do. I reached the decision a few days ago to honor my marriage while honoring my emerging sense of "me." I wear the rings on my right hand. It felt strange at first but no longer. My empty ring finger is symbolic of simply being a child of God, precious in God's sight—no one else's—because that is completion in itself.

PRAYER: *Good and gracious God, you love and accept me at all ages and stages. You bless my efforts to understand what it means to be alone and free to be myself, without a husband and the responsibilities of marriage. Grant me wisdom in my decision making. Amen.*

THOUGHT FOR THE DAY: Let's take the time to be silent and pay attention to our inner self.

TOMATOES AND HUMMERS

READ PSALM 69:30-32.

Let the oppressed see [God's saving power] and be glad;
you who seek God, let your hearts revive.

PSALM 69:32

After a seniors' exercise session at the gym, I decided to celebrate the beautiful spring day with a stop at the garden center. I planned to get replacement plants for the basket by my front door. The winter had battered the tender flowers in a way that reminded me of my own vulnerability to the cold wilderness of my widowhood. The sunny spring day brought a little stirring of new life, a bit of thaw in the icy grip of deep grief. Though I mourn my losses, I continue learning to live alone, learning to live anew. I lean into a path toward humble wisdom forced upon me by widowhood. To my surprise, I caught myself singing from a grateful heart.

For a time that afternoon, I even thanked God for my painful, bewildering journey. The experience of losing a beloved spouse is a demanding teacher. The bereavement invites me every day to learn about the depth of my faith and the breadth of God's love. It invites me to discover more about myself and my value as a child of God. Stripped of my role as wife, I can stand in the authentic simplicity of a loving relationship with God. Such validation and affirmation boggles my mind.

At the garden shop I bought a large clay pot and a strong, healthy Better Boy tomato plant with some tiny yellow blooms. Then I spotted hummingbird feeders and decided to buy one. Back home I fixed some sugar-water nectar and quickly put my purchases in place on the deck. The sun warmed my face and cheered my heart as I sat in my teal blue, plastic Adirondack chair admiring my environs. I dreamed about big, red, luscious tomatoes for BLT sandwiches, and I anticipated the arrival of tiny, iridescent green birds with ruby-throat patches darting and hovering around my new feeder. My appreciation for the magnificence of the universe arrived as a springtime gift after months of dogged perseverance and often perplexing passage through my first winter of grief.

PRAYER: *Gracious God, you reveal your love to me through simple gifts of sunshine, tomato plants, and hummingbirds. I may cry again tonight when I climb into my empty bed, but you will comfort my soul and invite me to peaceful rest and hope for tomorrow. Thank you. Amen.*

THOUGHT FOR THE DAY: How is God offering us gifts today?

SILVERSNEAKERS

READ 1 THESSALONIANS 5:23.

---

*May the God of peace himself sanctify you entirely; and may
your spirit and soul and body be kept sound and blameless
at the coming of our Lord Jesus Christ.*

1 THESSALONIANS 5:23

The tall, trim, tawny instructor stepped up on the low platform at the front of the large room, flipped on the music, and said, "Good morning, everybody. Time to get those heart rates up." With that cue, about forty seniors sitting in chairs began swinging their arms and pumping their legs to the beat of "You Make Me Feel So Young." The fifty-five-minute session included working with weights, basketballs, and stretch bands plus some aerobic movement. Often the friendly trainer teased the seniors during the workout. "How low can you go? Can you keep up with Bill? He's dancing down there." The amazing thing about Bill's prowess was his age—he's eighty-seven.

When January rolled around, eight months after Bob's death, my number one New Year's resolution was to find and participate regularly in an exercise program. Like many others who are caregivers for a dying spouse, I was guilty of self-neglect. I had even waited so long to get my retina surgery done during the months my husband had four surgeries, I now live with permanent blurred vision in my right eye. When we are living through "life and death" days, the last thing we think about is quirky eyesight. Such is the consequence of neglecting myself.

I kept my resolution, and what a difference SilverSneakers is making in my life. An online search led me to this fun, energizing program that helps older adults take greater control of their health by encouraging physical activity and educational seminars. Health

he country, including mine, offer this award-winning
ple who are eligible for Medicare for *free*. Benefits
ship in the fitness center with access to all programs
The senior classes, held three times weekly, are cus-
older adults who want to improve their strength, balance,
endurance, and flexibility. Our trained leader, a caring and friendly
man, knows each participant by name and inquires about his or her
well-being. He is so beloved by his seniors that his classes are packed
to maximum capacity.

When I entered the gym my first day, a woman named Myrtle
came up and took me under her wing. She showed me what to do,
set up a chair next to hers, and helped me find weights, a basketball,
and stretch bands. We became instant friends, and my circle of friends
continues to grow. Often after class, five, or as many as ten of us, go
out to a restaurant for lunch. We pray together, tell stories, and share
our incredible life experiences.

When I, a lonely widow struggling to build a new life, decided
to honor my body by enrolling in SilverSneakers, I discovered benefits
that far exceeded my wildest expectations. My body is getting stronger,
but more importantly I have found friends who also love the Lord.

PRAYER: *Loving and bountiful God, help me to care for my body in a
way that honors you. Thank you for the gifts of fun and friends who share
my pursuit of a healthy lifestyle. Amen.*

THOUGHT FOR THE DAY: We can serve God by taking care of
our bodies.

CAR CARE

*Do you not know that your body is a temple of the Holy
Spirit within you, which you have from God?*

1 CORINTHIANS 6:19

Only a fleet manager who sold thousands of police cars and trucks
of all sizes would think in terms of vehicle stewardship, but that is
precisely what my husband did for a living. As we drove down the
highway, Bob would comment on truck axles and the features of the
various vehicles he observed along the way. One thing annoyed him
immensely: seeing puffs of black smoke belched from poorly main-
tained trucks. I hear his deep voice in my head to this day: "All that's
required to stop that horrible pollution is a little routine maintenance
and new oil filters. They don't cost much. Such stupidity!"

I relived that scenario once more as I sat in the small waiting
room at Jiffy Lube. I had come there from the full-service car wash to
get the oil changed before a long drive to visit relatives in Mississippi.
I sensed Bob's approval of the way I remained a good steward of our
vehicle the way he had been.

Stewardship and responsibility push me to take care of other
possessions including this grieving heart of mine. I did not create the
body I inhabit, but I am in charge of taking care of it. God sent the
Son to redeem me in spirit, soul, and body.

I need to guard my body and my mind against the influences
of anxiety, doubt, fear, bitterness, worry, anger, prejudice, and com-
plaint. God loves this aging body of mine even with its limitations.
My responsibility is to give myself to the Lord—to open my inner
self and my spirit so that I may be filled with God's love and light. I
desperately need to be molded into God's image and to be responsible

for the maintenance of my physical and inner health. The payoff just might be a dependable vehicle for a long journey toward holiness, wholeness, and exquisite joy.

PRAYER: *Thank you, Generous Provider, for the gifts you have given. May I be a good steward of my possessions, including my body, so that all I have and all I am may be used for your glory. Amen.*

THOUGHT FOR THE DAY: God wants us to be good stewards of our possessions including our bodies.

LYME DISEASE

READ MATTHEW 9:20-22.

[The hemorrhaging woman] said to herself, "If I only touch his cloak, I will be healed." Jesus turned and saw her. "Take heart, daughter," he said, "your faith has healed you." And the woman was healed at that moment.

MATTHEW 9:21-22, NIV

My sister and I were enjoying a relaxing vacation on North Carolina's Outer Banks when I awakened one morning with a fiery rash. She searched the Internet and decided I had *bedbug bites*. The corner pharmacist looked at the red, itchy bumps and concluded that I had *sand flea bites*. Miserable but equipped with cortisone cream and Benadryl, we continued our plans for a Safari Jeep ride to see the wild horses and later to attend a production of "The Lost Colony." Back home I called my doctor, but because she had no openings, a resident saw me and determined I had *chigger bites*. Armed with a prescription for steroids, I returned home and crawled back into bed. My headache and fatigue were severe.

After a week with no improvement, I called my doctor again. She took one look at me and diagnosed Lyme Disease caused by an infected deer tick bite. She found the telltale bull's eye bite site on my back where I couldn't see it. The doctor said there has been a dramatic increase in these cases with the growth in the deer population, especially in the eastern United States. After two thirty-day rounds of a strong antibiotic, I began to recover, but the vestiges of severe headache, extreme fatigue, joint pain, and brain fog remained to some degree for three more months.

During this time I was hit by waves of grief that left me feeling vulnerable, fragile, and lonely. I missed my husband and our conversations. When we experience illness, every emotion intensifies. I cried often as I was forced to face the full implications of a loss that was irreversible and permanent. I remained faithful to my daily time of devotion, prayer, and scripture, and one morning I received a God-wink that moved me out of my grief and sped up my healing. The story appears in three of the Gospels.

A woman who has suffered hemorrhages for twelve years is considered unclean by her community and unfit for social interaction. She is not to be touched by any person simply because she is bleeding. Yet she has the temerity to touch the edge of Jesus' cloak because she believes she will be healed. It is a risk, a serious breach of religious and social norms, but she musters the courage to touch the edge (may have been the fringe or tassels at the corners) of Jesus' outer garment. Jesus does not scold or rebuke her but responds radically. He elevates the woman because of her faith.

This story reminds me that in times of utter desperation, we don't have to worry about the correct way to reach out to God. Like this woman we simply reach out in faith. God will respond. Though she is considered "unclean," God, through Jesus, changes the rules and calls her faithful. We too can be confident God will take care of us when we're sick and in need of healing.

PRAYER: *God who hears my prayers, I come with a full heart to thank you for healing me when I have been sick. Grant me the grace to be sensitive to those who are sick and to respond to their needs for support and prayer. Amen.*

THOUGHT FOR THE DAY: The healing love of God is always available to God's people.

BLEST BE THE TIE

Read Romans 15:5-7, 13.

---

*May the God of steadfastness and encouragement grant you
to live in harmony with one another.*

Romans 15:5

One of my favorite hymns from elementary years on is "Blest Be the Tie That Binds." It remains a favorite because the music and chords are simple and easy enough for a piano player with limited skill to master. A second reason is the profound simplicity I find in the way the song presents the nature of the Christian church:

> Blessed be the tie that binds our hearts in Christian love;
>> the fellowship of kindred minds is like to that above.
> Before our Father's throne we pour our ardent prayers;
>> our fears, our hopes, our aims are one, our comforts and
>> our cares.
> We share each other's woes, our mutual burdens bear;
>> and often for each other flows the sympathizing tear.
>> (UMH 557)

These first three verses certainly describe my experience of church. Through Bible studies, Stephen Ministry, committees, teaching adults and children, worship experiences, retreats, and fellowship opportunities, I have friends and "ties that bind" across decades and several states. I cannot imagine life without them.

Here's an example of a Christian friend who has enriched my life in recent days. Lynn and I met when she began to attend a women's weekly Bible study I facilitated, and our friendship only deepened when her husband died a few months after Bob did. She phoned this week from Texas to tell me about the death of a lovely woman of faith. Lynn told me about waking with a sense of urgency to go visit Mary Helen in rehab where she was recovering after a hospitalization with pneumonia. She hugged Mary Helen and told her how much she loved and valued her. Lynn said our friend was bedridden, weak, and unable to talk, but she communicated reciprocal feelings with her eyes. When Lynn left, she paused at the door and blew Mary Helen a kiss; Mary Helen was able to gesture a kiss in return. The next day Lynn got the call Mary Helen had died, and Lynn picked up the phone to share those precious moments with me. She told me about the obituary and how our dear friend had requested that in lieu of flowers or memorial donations, people should spend time with their friends and loved ones—a request symbolic of Mary Helen's life.

The support networks that we create for ourselves—Christian friend to friend, neighbor to neighbor, woman to woman, widow to widow—provide for strength, hope, encouragement, love, comfort, communion, and stability. In sharing ourselves with others, we find our happiness expanded, our sorrow lightened, and our mutual relationship with God deepened as a sacrament of love and life.

PRAYER: *With my heart filled with gratitude, I thank you, Lord God, for gifting me with good friends and the fellowship of Christians worldwide. These networks carry a rich and sacred trust. May this trust continue to grow this day and into eternity. Amen.*

THOUGHT FOR THE DAY: Blest be the tie that binds friends together.

A FRAGRANT OFFERING

READ 2 CORINTHIANS 2:14-16 AND EPHESIANS 5:1-2.

But thanks be to God, who in Christ always leads us in triumphal procession, and through us spreads in every place the fragrance that comes from knowing him. For we are the aroma of Christ to God.

2 CORINTHIANS 2:14-15

A group of church members were exploring the images of God found in scripture during a conference a couple of weeks ago with the Rev. Dr. Lauren Winner. One family of images we discussed had to do with God as a sensory being—perceiving with the senses. The psalmist asks, "He who planted the ear, does he not hear? He who formed the eye, does he not see?"(Ps. 94:9). The more we played with the idea of God and the five senses of sight, hearing, touch, taste, and smell, more examples started popping off the pages of our Bibles like a dozen bags of Orville Redenbacher popcorn exploding all at once. The exercise was energizing and enriching.

Pondering God's sense of smell became especially intriguing. We chanted a hymn based on Psalm 141, and this line still haunts my daily life: "Let my prayer rise up like incense before you." According to Exodus 30:7, priests offered incense on the altar every morning. How wonderful to think that our prayers are also an incense offering made to delight and tickle God's olfactory sense!

The passage from Second Corinthians presents a picture of Christ's followers taking on a special fragrance simply by knowing him, by being in his presence. In that scenario, the disciples become the aroma of Jesus Christ to God. Smell is powerful; it can be a way of communicating, of communion, of warning, of evoking memories of a person or an event. In Ephesians 5:1-2, Paul describes Jesus on the cross emitting an aroma: "Therefore be imitators of God, as beloved children, and live in love, as Christ loved us and gave himself up for us, a fragrant offering and sacrifice to God." We are to imitate with prayer and self-offering—actions that have the power to reconnect us to God.

Each person has a unique smell. Bob's dog wanted to hang out on his bed or in his bathroom for days after he died. I have a widow friend who wore her husband's T-shirts to bed to keep his smell present. One little boy I know went to bed with one of his father's T-shirts after his dad deployed to Afghanistan. Police will use a piece of clothing to trigger a search dog's hunt for a missing person. Not all smells are pleasant, and some may linger for a very long time. After my friend's house burned, she remarked often that the hardest part about the experience was the awful smell that would not go away.

If I have the option of choosing my personal smell, I would select one created by years and years of hanging out with Christ. How lovely if our prayers go up like incense to soothe, comfort, and delight God!

PRAYER: *O God, O God, my Lord, let my prayers rise before you as incense. May I be a sweet, sweet fragrance in your kingdom. Amen.*

THOUGHT FOR THE DAY: May we bring the aroma of Christ to others today.

UNIQUELY MADE

READ PSALM 139:13-18.

For it was you who formed my inward parts;
you knit me together in my mother's womb.
I praise you, for I am fearfully and wonderfully made.

PSALM 139:13-14

In the scripture passage above, the psalmist expresses something it has taken me a long time to own at the center of my being. He understands that his own creation is as wondrous as the other great deeds of the Lord. The Lord's great deeds include me and my creation; I too am uniquely and wonderfully made. But sadly most of us get bruised early in life by the hideous unfairness and injustice that humiliates and demeans a child for something beyond his or her control. Many girls are not taken seriously or given equal treatment because of their gender. Some boys have struggled to meet their parents' expectations of masculinity regardless of how unrealistic and insensitive they may be. Children quickly learn if their hair is too straight or too curly, if they are good at sports or lack physical prowess, if they are too small or too big, if they are quick students or have trouble with school. These rankings and comparisons start right after birth, and we internalize the feedback we receive from day one. Children are like little sponges, and they quickly soak up if they are loved or unlovable, valued or considered unworthy.

As I prepared a Bible study on Matthew, I was struck again with how dearly Jesus loves and values little children. (See Matthew 19:13-15.) I went to the bookcase and retrieved a small clay figurine of Jesus seated with small children around him given to me years ago by my dearest friend, Emily. I set it next to the "Christ candle" I light at the beginning of each class. During the course of the lesson we talked about God's compassion, mercy, and the unconditional love we call grace. I shared an example given in Philip Yancey's book, *What's So Amazing About Grace?*, which he cited from the movie *Ironweed*. Characters played by Jack Nicholson and Meryl Streep, drunk, stumbled upon an old Eskimo woman, lying in the snow.

"Is she drunk or a bum?" asks Nicholson.
"Just a bum. Been one all her life."
"And before that?"
"She was a whore in Alaska."
"She hasn't been a whore all her life. Before that?"
"I dunno. Just a little kid, I guess."
"Well, a little kid's something. It's not a bum and it's not a whore. It's something. Let's take her in."*

Societies around the world for centuries have promoted the bias that children and older adults—including widows—are dispensable. That idea is pure insanity, and I hope none of us buys into the notion that we are inferior in any way as we enter this new life of widowhood. Let's strip all old baggage away and resume the attitude of a loved child, wonderfully and uniquely made in God's image.

PRAYER: *Thank you, God, for creating me and for loving me unconditionally. Amen.*

THOUGHT FOR THE DAY: We are wonderfully made, unique manifestations of God's creation.

*Philip Yancy, *What's So Amazing About Grace?* (Grand Rapids, MI: Zondervan Publishing House, 1997), 280.

MOURNING
TO
MORNING

*Sing praises to the L*ORD*, O you his faithful ones,*
and give thanks to his holy name.
For his anger is but for a moment;
his favor is for a lifetime.
Weeping may linger for the night,
but joy comes with the morning.

PSALM 30:4-5

DINING ALONE

READ PSALM 118:1, 24, 28-29.

This is the day that the LORD has made;
let us rejoice and be glad in it.

PSALM 118:24

Often widows without children at home will express to me that one of the most unpleasant results of losing a spouse is dining alone. Mealtime was special to my husband and me, and we most especially appreciated suppertime together. It was a big loss, even though I often dine with a neighbor, family, and friends.

I was blessed by something that happened recently when I fixed a meal for a widow who had surgery the day before. I took a little vase of flowers for our centerpiece and set the table with flowered napkins to add to the festivity of our meal together. She was surprised by my actions and said that in her native country of Sweden, no one would do what I was doing. The government takes care of people, but this kind of neighbor-to-neighbor caring would not occur. Growing up in the South, it only seemed natural to me.

As we talked about living alone, she told me, in her soft, lilting Swedish accent, a story her Norwegian husband had told her decades ago. While in graduate school in Amsterdam in 1937, he lived in a tiny apartment over a store. There was another small apartment across the hall that was occupied by a diminutive Jewish man who had fled Nazi Germany. The graduate student was intrigued by something the man did every evening. He would cook his supper on his small hot plate and set the tiny table, big enough for only one diner, with tablecloth, candle, silverware, and plate. He would put on his hat and coat and go into the hall and close the door. Then he would knock gently on the door and proceed to reenter his apartment and sit at his table for dinner. He was his own respected dinner guest.

Like my friend's husband, I was intrigued by this behavior and wished I could ask the man what he was thinking. What did his actions symbolize for him? As I reflected on the story, I realized I had started doing something similar. I set my table with tablecloth, flowers, candle, and cloth napkin in a pewter napkin ring. I pour my beverage in a fancy little glass or cheery cup. I say grace and enjoy my meals with reverence and gratitude. My little ritual includes reciting, "This is the day that the LORD has made; let us rejoice and be glad in it." No more are the days of standing at the sink and eating on the run.

In a collection of poems by Billy Collins, former Poet Laureate of the United States and also New York State, titled *Aimless Love*, I found a delightful poem called "Dining Alone." He writes, "I have brought neither book nor newspaper / since reading material is considered cheating."* I'm learning to be more comfortable eating alone, but I'm not quite there yet. I still turn on my TV to the evening local and world news.

PRAYER: *God who fills my life with good things, I rejoice in the abundance I are learning to find in my solitude. Thank you. Amen.*

THOUGHT FOR THE DAY: God's love is unchanging in the midst of changing circumstances.

*Billy Collins, *Aimless Love: New and Selected Poems* (New York: Random House, 2013), 239.

ONE RED STOCKING

READ JOHN 1:1-5.

What has come into being in [Jesus] was life, and the life was the light of all people. The light shines in the darkness, and the darkness did not overcome it.

JOHN 1:3-5

The second Christmas without my husband loomed large, dark, and cold. The words of a hymn swirled around my heart and hearth over and over again: "In the bleak midwinter, frosty wind made moan" (UMH 221). I had added insulation to the condo a few weeks earlier, so I knew the shivering came from within my spirit and mind and not from the icy weather outdoors. The shortest days of the year further reflected the darkness and sadness of my mood. It was Advent—supposedly a time of joyous preparation and expectancy as we await the Bethlehem Babe. I decided to fake it, to overrule my gloom, and so I went to the large hall closet and pulled out the plastic bins of Christmas decorations.

The decision had been made earlier not to put up the large tree for the first time in memory because I planned to travel out of state to be with my ninety-five-year-old mother. Even so, with a busy schedule, it took six days to get the decorations in place. I purchased seven white pillar candles that I put on a metal tray and surrounded them with sprigs of red holly berries. I set the tray and candles in the large, empty fireplace. I made one last addition. I hung one red stocking from the mantel—one lonely, limp, empty, solitary, forlorn, red stocking.

I fixed a cup of hot chocolate with a generous handful of peppermint marshmallows thinking it would cheer me up. I lit the fireplace candles and settled down in my armchair with the colorful, ceramic Christmas mug of steaming cocoa. Light and warmth permeated the room with such intensity I forgot to be sad. To my surprise I found myself embracing my widowhood and aloneness. I became aware I had reached a turning point in my grief. I shifted my focus from the empty, red stocking to the dancing lights of the fireplace candles and took another sip of hot chocolate.

I began to ponder ways I could creatively shine the Christ child's light into my world. How might I be a channel of helpfulness for others? I imagined filling my stocking with small signs of faith and love: a kind word, smiles, a helping hand, tiny gifts given freely, listening ears, turning the other cheek, an open mind, a compassionate heart, songs of praise, prayers for healing, words of encouragement, greeting cards, "comfort" meals, phone calls, blankets for the shelter, a man's warm coat.

The frosty wind moans "in the bleak midwinter," and darkness comes earlier in shortened days. Into this needy world, God sent a Holy Child to herald hope. I began to sing the fourth verse of "In the Bleak Midwinter": "What can I give him, poor as I am? If I were a shepherd, I would bring a lamb; if I were a Wise Man, I would do my part; yet what I can I give him: give my heart" (UMH 221).

And so I picture myself giving him one red stocking filled to overflowing with "this little light of mine." As my Irish husband used to say, "Happy Christmas, one and all."

PRAYER: *God of light and love, life may not be what it used to be, but the best days have not come and gone with the loss of my spouse. May I be a vessel of love, hope, and healing so that in you I may find fullness of joy this Christmastide. Amen.*

THOUGHT FOR THE DAY: When we respond to God's call, any day becomes a blessing.

AT TABLE

READ ACTS 2:46-47.

Day by day, as [the believers] spent much time together in the temple, they broke bread at home and ate their food with glad and generous hearts, praising God and having the goodwill of all the people.

ACTS 2:46-47

I spent ten days over the Christmas and New Year's holidays with my ninety-five-year-old mother who routinely shared her meals with three other residents at a table for four. With me, a fifth person on the scene, the arrangement was disrupted. Sometimes one of them would have to sit somewhere else, sometimes I would pull up a chair and sit at the corner, or sometimes my mother and I would move to a different table. Conversation was often about the way things "used to be." One thing the residents missed was having avocados to eat. And so I went out the next day and bought each one a ripe avocado. Their smiles were big.

During my visit there, I stayed at my brother's lake house in the woods some twenty-five miles away. He and his wife had gone skiing with children and grandkids, so I was alone every morning. I sat at the table looking out huge floor-to-ceiling windows, watching the shifting natural setting as birds flew to the feeders, wind ruffled the pine needles, and lake water danced in the dawning sunlight. The Spirit hovered around me, and I never felt alone.

Christmas Eve I attended a candlelight midnight mass at the little church where I was confirmed and all three of my children were baptized. I knew few people after living away these many decades, and yet the familiar scriptures, traditional music, and eucharistic meal offered a feeling of tribal homecoming as together we welcomed the Christ child.

Three days later I phoned Millie, a former neighbor, and asked if we could visit over a cup of coffee as we often did when I came to town to visit Mother. We had raised our children together for a number of years and had remained close friends even after I moved away. We both lost our husbands in 2012 and were struggling with being widows while also being relieved that the long years of caregiving were behind us. Millie decided we would have coffee at her house the next afternoon.

As I was parking my car, two other former neighbors walked up, and a sweet reunion began. The table for four was set with pretty napkins, plates of cheesecake slices, and a pot of steaming coffee. We took turns catching up on our lives and sharing stories of what had happened with husbands and children in the intervening years. One had met the serious challenge of cancer. Some children had struggled with various problems. Grandchildren had blessed and some brought worries. Four women of faith shared a three-hour agape meal.

Agape is a Koine Greek word and the main word used for love in the New Testament. Agape love meals were part of a loosely structured early Christian service held in homes (not a Eucharist but a social meal much like a coffee hour after worship). Each person would bring what little food he or she had to share, and they would sit around, tell stories of what God was doing in their lives, and encourage one another in the faith. God's table, whether set for one or many, manifests experiences of community and selfless, unconditional love. Thanks be to God.

PRAYER: *Blessed are you, Lord God, for you give me food to sustain my life and community to gladden my heart, through Jesus Christ the Lord. Amen.*

THOUGHT FOR THE DAY: Every meal offers us an opportunity to celebrate God's goodness.

IN HIS HONOR

READ I THESSALONIANS 5:11, 14-15.

Therefore encourage one another and build up each other,
as indeed you are doing.

I THESSALONIANS 5:11

In 1964, a Canadian Royal Navy officer by the name of Jean Vanier changed the way we look at community with the mentally disabled. He invited two men from a nearby asylum to come live with him at his home in a small French village north of Paris. He named the little community *L'Arche* (French for "ark," a symbol of refuge and deliverance) and thereby started a federation of 146 communities in thirty-five countries on six continents.* There are eighteen, plus three emerging, communities in the United States.

Vanier saw his plan as the opportunity of a lifetime, an invitation "to go down the social ladder, not up." He felt that the greatest desire of persons with handicapping conditions and all human beings was for community. He made the observation that together with persons with disabilities, "We can let down the barriers and turn our backs on the need for power. We can discover that life is to be celebrated together, where the weak and the strong can sing and dance together."**

Henri Nouwen, internationally renowned priest, author, and professor, spent the last eleven years of his life in L'Arche communities—one year in Trosly, France, and ten years at L'Arche Daybreak, Canada. Nouwen found meaning for his life living among those with intellectual disabilities. God often surprises us by turning conventions and expectations upside down.

I thought about the juxtaposition of weak and strong, able-bodied and physically handicapped, when I read an article about Nouwen and L'Arche. A couple of days later I received a request to help with summer camp scholarships for physically or mentally challenged children. My husband was from a large Irish Catholic family with limited resources. He repeatedly recalled, with great appreciation, his scholarship to attend a Salvation Army summer camp. A lightbulb came on. That's it. That's how I can honor him. Every year a child will go to summer camp on a scholarship in my husband's memory. He would be thrilled to know we are encouraging and building up another dear child of God.

PRAYER: *God of song and dance and summer camps, multiply my gifts and use them for the nurture and affirmation of children with disabilities and their caregivers. Teach me that power and strength are found in love and community. Amen.*

THOUGHT FOR THE DAY: May we practice encouragement, affirmation, and building up one another.

*Jean Vanier, "Where the Weak and Strong Dance Together," in Bob Abernathy and William Bole, *The Life of Meaning: Reflections on Faith, Doubt, and Repairing the World* (New York: Seven Stories Press, 2007), 371.
**Ibid., 375.

ON THE MOUNTAIN

READ EXODUS 3:1-6.

---

*Then Moses said, "I must turn aside and look at this great
sight, and see why the bush is not burned up." . . . Then
[God] said, "Come no closer! Remove the sandals from your
feet, for the place on which you are standing is holy ground."*

EXODUS 3:3, 5

Do strange things happen on mountains? I imagine Moses would
double over with laughter if you asked him that question. He might
tell you about his experience tending his father-in-law Jethro's flock in
the wilderness and coming upon "the mountain of God." The angel of
the Lord appears in a flame of fire coming from a bush that is blazing
but not consumed. When he goes to check out this incredible sight,
God speaks from the bush and tells him to remove his sandals for he
is standing on holy ground. When Moses asks for God's name, God
says, "I AM WHO I AM" (Exod. 3:14). Wow! What's going on? It doesn't
make sense, especially not to modern readers. How could a bush be
on fire but not be consumed?

I read this story as if it were an imaginative retelling of an internal
experience, namely the act of being called by God to a vocation, and
there is no need to explain the miracle of the burning bush scientif-
ically. Whatever Moses sees with the naked eye does not matter; he
understands it to be a sign that he is in the presence of the Holy. The
place where he is standing is a sanctuary, a sacred place where sandals
must be removed. It is here that Moses will reluctantly answer God's
call to liberate the Hebrew slaves in Egypt, a feat at the very heart of
Israel's historical faith.

Scripture is filled with strange mountain experiences. Another
example is the mysterious and fascinating narrative of the Transfigu-

ration of Jesus. Jesus takes Peter, James, and John with him up a high mountain and suddenly Moses and Elijah appear and are talking with Jesus. God speaks from a cloud, "This is my Son, the Beloved; with him I am well pleased; listen to him!" (Matt. 17:5). Jesus orders them not to be afraid and to tell no one about the vision.

A couple of weeks ago I gave myself the gift of two days and nights at an Episcopal conference center in the North Carolina mountains. I was fighting the winter doldrums and thought the change of scenery might break my feelings of "stuckness," but I really had no expectations and was unsure why I wanted to go. It had been twenty-three years since my last visit to the center, and after settling into my cabin, I walked through snowdrifts to the outdoor Saint Francis Chapel. I knew immediately that I had returned to holy ground and a sanctuary where I had experienced a theophany (a manifestation of God's presence) many years ago. All the troubles, struggles, pain, changes, and transitions of widowhood melted away like the melting snow running down the brook under the small wooden bridge beneath my snow boots. I felt liberated from my personal history and stood there in the rustic sanctuary empty of everything but God.

The next morning I looked out my window, and two tree limbs had formed a V above a snowbank. Framed by and centered in the V in the distance, I could see the white cross on the far side of the lake. I fell to my knees in thanksgiving. Strange and beautiful things happen on mountains. They open Moses, Peter, James, John, and me to the mystery and glory of God.

PRAYER: *Living God of miraculous manifestations, may I hear you when you call and respond with faithful discipleship. Amen.*

THOUGHT FOR THE DAY: May we open our eyes to see God everywhere today.

GIVE 'EM YOUR SOCKS

READ MATTHEW 5:1-3, 6-8, 40-42.

"Blessed are the poor in spirit, for theirs is the kingdom of heaven. . . . If anyone wants to sue you and take your coat, give your cloak as well."

MATTHEW 5:3, 40

As my husband's health problems increased, I cut back on my activities outside of the home. One that I missed terribly was being a part of a Bible study. As my grief eased, I longed for study group, and the search for one led me to a group that was actually using the exact same materials I had been studying in my Texas group before I dropped out. I was thrilled, but the group disbanded when summer came. In late August a call came to the church office inquiring about someone who might lead a Bible study at a retirement community. I was asked to facilitate and soon began a study of the Gospel of Matthew with a small group of remarkable people.

Without question, the Sermon on the Mount (Matthew 5:1–7:29) is one of the most-studied, analyzed, discussed, and pondered portions of scripture throughout the centuries. Its message continues to confound and challenge readers, myself included. As Jesus sits (the posture of a teacher, someone with authority) on a gently sloping hillside by the Sea of Galilee, he does not offer moral maxims or a new legal code to be enforced by the church. He describes instead a picture of what the inner character of the followers of Jesus in any age should be. He instructs those who, with him, will be about the business of building the kingdom of God, fulfilling God's dream of life and community under the gracious rule of God. The teachings are Jesus' call for his people to love God and to "love thy neighbour as thyself" (Mark 12:31, KJV)—without reservation.

While reading *A Guide to Prayer for All Who Walk with God*, I came across a story of another Wednesday night Bible study group that was also studying Matthew's Gospel. Janet Wolf tells the story of John, a homeless man living at the downtown mission. John woke up one night to find his shoes missing. He pulled out his knife and went looking, walking up and down the dining hall, table by table. In his former life, he was mean. Folks knew it, and he didn't care. He yelled, threatened, swore, and hollered. "It's one thing to give up drinking and drugging. It's another thing when they steal your shoes," he cried.

Jim, another member of the Bible study group living at the mission, began to holler from the other side of the dining room, "Bible says if they take one cloak give them your other one; if they took your shoes, give 'em your socks. Put that knife away and give 'em your socks."

John concluded his story this way: "Folded up my knife. Took a long time doing it too. Walked barefoot to the service center this morning—got me some more shoes—but ain't it hard to live this stuff out!"*

John and Jim understand what it means to be "poor in spirit." I'm in awe of these men and also how Bible study radically transforms our hearts and our inner lives. I am grateful I now have the time and freedom to study again. I miss Bob, but the gifts of my new life invite me to a deeper spirituality—to gifts that also heal my lonely heart.

PRAYER: *God of grace and mercy, grant me poverty of soul that I may be empty to receive you and your will for my days on earth, so that I have the vulnerability to "give 'em my socks" and lighten my neighbor's need. Amen.*

THOUGHT FOR THE DAY: How can we love others as Jesus loves us?

*Janet Wolf, *A Guide to Spiritual Discernment*, Rueben P. Job, compiler, excerpted in Rueben P. Job, Norman Shawchuck, John S. Mogabgab, *A Guide to Prayer for All Who Walk with God* (Nashville, TN: Upper Room Books, 2013), 41-42.

THE CHICKENS

READ 2 CORINTHIANS 1:3-7.

Praise be to the God and Father of our Lord Jesus Christ . . .
who comforts us in all our troubles, so that we can comfort
those in any trouble with the comfort we ourselves receive
from God.

2 CORINTHIANS 1:3-4, NIV

The hospice social worker, chaplain, volunteers, nurses, and aides had a profound influence on my husband, me, our friends, and family during Bob's last days. I sing praises to the highest heavens for the way they brought compassion, sensitivity, professionalism, dignity, and respect to Bob and to each of us throughout those days. My dream became to one day be able to do what they had done for me for someone else going through the hospice experience.

Eighteen months after Bob's death, my pastor called and asked if I would be willing to visit a family whose mother had been placed in hospice with a life expectancy of four to six months. The blessings that have come to me from this one volunteer ministry defy limits and description.

The daughter, around forty years old, is a secretary at a university, and her husband, a leg amputee, has a job as a security guard at a large manufacturing company. She is Filipino and he American. They met on the Internet, and after several visits decided to get married and live in the States. Two years ago the young couple decided to move her aging parents (she is an only child) to live with them in North Carolina. In recent months the mother, Edith, was diagnosed with heart disease and kidney failure. The case is further complicated because she is not a US citizen and has no insurance. A faithful God assures us our every need will be supplied, and this little family can attest to that truth as they have been able to acquire medical treatment and resources. They are doing a heroic job of providing loving devotion and steadfast care for Edith at home. When I am in prayer at Edith's bedside with her daughter and husband standing behind me, I feel the presence of angels looking on and anointing us in ways that defy words.

The large yard provides space for the father to farm and grow vegetables and flowers. He's also a proficient carpenter, and these skills are helping him stay busy while he devotedly attends to the needs of his dying wife. He has recently been given four hens and a rooster. While admiring his beautifully made pen with roosting cubicles, I asked if he planned to name his chickens, and he chuckled. On my next visit, I inquired about his naming the chickens, and he got an enormous grin on his face. Then he told me, "The rooster is named Tiger Woods—lover, you know." His grin grew even bigger. I asked, "What about the hens?" He replied, "Two of them hum all the time like they are singing, so I named one Celine and the other one Beyoncé. The brown one I named Oprah. My son-in-law suggested I name the fourth for someone in the Philippines, so I named that one Ai-Ai for a comedian there." I said, "Now let me be sure I have the names correct. They are Tiger Woods, Celine, Beyoncé, Oprah, and Ai-Ai." The room filled with the music of our giggles.

Gladness and laughter are not attained by eradicating pain and suffering. Joy is not an escape from sorrow. But humor, a light heart, and the joy of the Lord give power to rise above grief and sadness in all situations.

PRAYER: *Thank you, Lord of laughter, for the blessing of new friends and funny moments. May those who have grieved find many opportunities to serve others going through times of loss and sadness. Amen.*

THOUGHT FOR THE DAY: Acts of service for others are also acts of love for Jesus.

BUDDIES

READ 1 JOHN 4:7-12.

No one has ever seen God; but if we love one another, God lives in us and his love is made complete in us.

1 JOHN 4:12, NIV

The phone rang, piercing my morning meditative reverie. No one calls that early so I knew immediately something was wrong. The caller was a dear friend informing me that Bob's best friend, Richard, had died two days earlier. She only found out when she was asked to assist with the lunch after his memorial service. The news hit me hard. It opened a flood of tears and deep grief for this truly good man whose devoted friendship and ministry to my husband over many years was inspirational and priceless.

The interdenominational organization called Stephen Ministry equips people to provide free, confidential, Christian, one-on-one care to those who are experiencing some form of life crisis. Bob and I had become friends with Richard through a Sunday school class. One night at a Stephen Ministry supervision meeting, someone asked if I thought Bob would like to have a Stephen Minister. No sooner had I enthusiastically endorsed the idea than Richard volunteered to be a Stephen Minister for my husband. Bob's illness was chronic, and his body was steadily deteriorating. In a matter of weeks these two men developed one of the most incredible relationships I've ever witnessed.

Richard sat by my husband's bedside for hours and hours, day after day as Bob lay dying. He read the above scripture at Bob's memorial service and made his special brownies for the reception. His unconditional love and steadfast friendship over many years of illness was authentically Christlike and an inspiring gift to all who witnessed it. Richard always inquired about how I was doing, and he blessed me too with his caring ministry.

A few days after Bob died, Richard and his lovely wife treated me and other family members to a delightful meal on the patio of a Mexican restaurant in Fort Worth. As we walked back to the parking lot, Richard came up to me and said, "Nell, Bob is the one who died, not you. Please remember to keep on living."

It took more than a week before I could write Richard's widow and pass along his wise words. My fond hope is that we two widows will honor those two buddies by carrying their love with us as we strive to live the rest of our lives gracefully and well.

PRAYER: *Lord God, I give you thanks for faith-filled friends who journey with me and show me your love. Amen.*

THOUGHT FOR THE DAY: May we live every minute of life with love, grace, and gratitude.

EAT THIS BREAD

READ EPHESIANS 1:17-23.

---

*And [God] has put all things under [Jesus'] feet and has
made him the head over all things for the church, which is
his body, the fullness of him who fills all in all.*

EPHESIANS 1:22-23

Sunday mornings spent at church have been my favorite moments of
the week since my earliest memories. God gave me an incredible gift
when my husband Bob shared my enthusiasm for Sunday morning
worship with our church family. Faithfully we attended together—
Bob's motorized wheelchair at the end of the pew with me sitting
alongside. Even on days when the pain was excruciating, Bob wanted
to be in the Lord's house on Sunday mornings and special holy days.
He soaked up every minute (although he slept through sermons), sang
with gusto, and held a special affinity for the Lord's Supper. Servers
would bring the bread and small plastic cup of juice to his chair, and
often we would get teary watching his determined struggle to take
Communion. The support of the people of Saint Barnabas United
Methodist Church in Arlington, Texas, and its people played a key
role in our lives for many years.

When I moved to North Carolina, I had a difficult time finding
a church where I felt at home, and I had to really work at finding a
place of belonging. Although the grief process hindered my progress,
after some months I decided to simply choose a church and jump in.
I became involved in three committees, volunteered for suppers at
Urban Ministries, attended programs, and joined the new member
class. Soon I began to know people and learn more about the unique
church I had joined. The congregation at Duke University Chapel
is an ecumenical Christian community with its own staff, council,

budget, and programs. There are 525 members with no buildings and no denominational governance, unusual for sure.

Recently the church hosted an overnight retreat at a lovely conference center on Caraway Mountain near Asheboro, North Carolina. The schedule included both work and play opportunities centered around the twofold task of building community and developing a vision for the future. Session discussions built upon passages from Ephesians, and the one above really intrigued me. The church's greatest title is "the body of Christ," and Christ, the head of the church, holds the highest spiritual power in the cosmos ("the fullness of him who fills all in all"). The head sustains, guides, inspires, enables, and strengthens, but it must have a body through which it can work.

As a church body there is one thing we do quite well: worship. My church's retreat closed at a lakeside outdoor chapel among sun-dappled trees. The children sang; the congregation read scriptures and offered prayers. When it came time for the Lord's Supper, we formed a circle and passed the bread and cup from person to person while singing "Eat This Bread" until everyone had shared in the Feast. A little toddler next to me began clapping his hands, and I joined in. Soon everyone was clapping and praising with a joyful, exuberant spirit. I had found where I belonged.

PRAYER: *Thank you, most gracious God, for a church where I may worship and serve you. May I use the gifts you have given for the building of your kingdom. Amen.*

THOUGHT FOR THE DAY: We are members of the body of Christ; may we grow together in faith.

TWENTY-FIVE CENT CONNECTION

READ EPHESIANS 2:4-10.

---

*By grace you have been saved through faith, and this is
not your own doing; it is the gift of God—not the result of
works, so that no one may boast. For we are what he has
made us, created in Christ Jesus for good works, which God
prepared beforehand to be our way of life.*

EPHESIANS 2:8-10

In the book of Ephesians, Paul writes using powerful, poetic language, and he encourages Christian churches and their members to a new life of unity, truth, love, and forgiveness. Every time I read the vision and prayers in these six short chapters, I marvel at God's sweeping plan for salvation and the exalted role of the church as a Spirit-filled community that brings the power and presence of the Lord to the world. The language soars and evokes a renewed commitment to sharing God's love story every day that I live.

When my grief was at its darkest, life seemed to be all about me, my loss, and the changes I was being forced to make. *Awful, yucky*—these words don't begin to describe those early weeks. Slowly, very slowly, deep grief lifted. I began to understand Bob's death not as an end but as a shift in meaning and responsibility.

One morning while I was sitting in my prayer chair, I looked down at my empty hands, weathered with age, covered with brown spots. They had held my husband's hand and been kissed in many a gallant display of his affection. They looked empty, but the notion hit me that in reality they are God's instruments full of love, grace, and a lifetime of memories. My hands were not designed for busyness or to fill a hole in my heart or to help me run from grief. God designed my hands for expressing love, grace, mercy, community, connection, prayer, and praise. And so I began a ritual every morning asking the Lord to open my eyes to see the needs of others and how I might show God's love to someone that day.

I resumed volunteering for Meals on Wheels in North Carolina as I had in Texas and Mississippi. Recently I told a lovely elderly woman in a wheelchair that I would be away visiting my ninety-five- year-old mother. In a rich melodic voice she said, "Be sure to let me know when you go, honey, because I want to give you twenty-five cents. You might get hungry and need to buy some Nabs." I kissed that sweet, wrinkled forehead and felt I had kissed the face of Jesus.

The years since Bob died have forged a new capacity for making connections between my own heart and the hearts of others. I am learning to connect more and more with the depth of God's love, and it is far deeper, broader, and wider than anything I could have imagined. It comes with a price tag of "twenty-five cents."

PRAYER: *Ever-gracious God, I know that you work all things together for good when love for you shapes my thoughts and actions. Open my eyes to see the connections you desire me to make with my neighbors. Amen.*

THOUGHT FOR THE DAY: In what tangible ways can we help others today?

BEST FRIEND

READ RUTH 1:16-18 AND JOHN 15:13-15.

-----

*"Do not press me to leave you
or to turn back from following you!
Where you go, I will go;
where you lodge, I will lodge."*

RUTH 1:16

The book of Ruth has been a favorite for as long as I can remember. Ruth, whose name appropriately means "friendship," was a Moabite living at the time of the Judges (between 1250 and 1050 BCE). Moabites, considered to be half-breeds and traditional enemies of the Israelites, came from an area east of the Dead Sea. Naomi and her family move there from Bethlehem to escape famine. One of Naomi's sons marries Ruth but dies young, leaving her childless. Ruth's love for her mother-in-law leads her to accept the traditions and religion of her adopted people and to return to Israel after Naomi is widowed. "Your God is mine," Ruth declares, "Death alone can part us" (Ruth 1:16-17, AP). What a remarkable friendship—"until death do us part."

God blessed me with that kind of friend, one who loved and cherished me and is now separated only by death. It is good to remember my husband and to wish the other side of the bed were not empty. I miss his deep voice telling me corny jokes followed by "Get it?" and his running commentary on what we were watching on TV. If I let myself dwell too long on the heartache and circumstances beyond my control, I could become sad and bitter. However, I am convinced God created me to enjoy life, and God gifted me with another best friend.

Each day I am invited to share my life with Jesus. I give that relationship time through prayer, scripture, study, communion, and community. Living consciously in his presence, I can face whatever pleasures, disappointments, adventures, or hardships each day brings. Eternal reality permeates this multidimensional, down-to-earth friendship. Walking hand in hand with the King of kings turns sorrow into joy, ashes into beauty, grief into dance. I feel an overwhelming desire to express my love to my Lord through gratitude and praise. This friendship will never end; we will never be parted—not even in death.

PRAYER: *What a friend you are, dear Lord, and I thank you for giving me life and all the blessings I enjoy every day. May my gratitude cultivate a loving spirit within me so that others may see your love and grace at work, not only in my life but in theirs as well. Amen.*

THOUGHT FOR THE DAY: Christ calls us to new hope and new life.

BOUNCEABILITY

READ PHILIPPIANS 3:12-14.

This one thing I do: forgetting what lies behind and straining forward to what lies ahead, I press on toward the goal for the prize of the heavenly call of God in Christ Jesus.

PHILIPPIANS 3:13-14

A cold front came through last night and brought a temporary end to the oppressive summer heat. My dog Molly and I appreciated the cool crisp air during our morning walk. I love standing on the side of a hill and looking down our path where rays from the rising sun filter through the leafy overhead bower. We always pause while I recite aloud one of my favorite scriptures: "The steadfast love of the LORD never ceases, his mercies never come to an end; they are new every morning; great is your faithfulness" (Lam. 3:22-23). Even on sad and challenging days, when I come here and take a deep breath, I am reminded of God's gifts of love, mercy, and grace. I am unable to stifle the grateful praises that bubble up from my soul.

After the refreshing walk, I poured a mug of hot coffee and went to my "Prayer Chair" for morning devotions, scripture, and writing journal entries. More than two years have passed since Bob's death. I began to reflect on the journey and realized that, with God's help and the love of family and friends, I had bounced through a season of heavy grief into a time when I learned to embrace the pain, the loneliness, the change. My mourning became a natural part of each day—a kind of tribute or memorial to my deceased husband. I continued to pray and bounce through time until I found myself making an even better tribute to Bob by loving life and others more fully because Bob had loved and cherished me.

Last night I finished reading *The Gifts of Imperfection: Let Go of Who You Think You're Supposed to Be and Embrace Who You Are* by Brené Brown, a research professor and writer whose lectures on courage, vulnerability, worthiness, and shame have been viewed by millions. In the chapter titled, "Cultivating a Resilient Spirit: Letting Go of Numbing and Powerlessness," Dr. Brown analyzes her data from thousands of interviews. She discovers factors that help people cope with stress and trauma and allow them to move forward in their lives while others seem stuck and unable to find their way past the trauma to meet the challenge and change it brought. Many are unable to say, "This hurts, this is tough, but I can get through it." Dr. Brown writes the following:

> According to the people I interviewed, . . . the things that made them bouncy—was their spirituality. . . . Without exception, spirituality—the belief in connection, a power greater than self, and interconnections grounded in love and compassion—emerged as a component of resilience. . . . Practicing spirituality is what brings healing and creates resilience. For me, spirituality is about connecting with God.*

Like the apostle Paul we press on because we hear God in nature, music, community, prayers, and scripture. God whispers, "I am beside you to bless you and to help you. Tell that to yourself over and over again until you start to bounce and your heart sings for joy."

PRAYER: *Thank you, loving and generous Father God, for the gift of bounceability. Use me to help others find courage and hope to press forward in their lives. Amen.*

THOUGHT FOR THE DAY: Practicing spirituality creates resilience and brings healing.

*Brené Brown, *The Gifts of Imperfection: Let Go of Who You Think You're Supposed to Be and Embrace Who You Are* (Center City, Minnesota: Hazelden, 2010), 64, 74.

POWERFUL WORDS

Read Isaiah 43:1-4.

Do not fear, for I have redeemed you;
I have called you by name, you are mine.
When you pass through the waters, I will be with you; . . .
Because you are precious in my sight,
and honored, and I love you.

Isaiah 43:1-2, 4

In the mid-1980s I visited my daughter who lived in Arlington, Virginia, at the time. She made reservations and treated me to a tour of the National Cathedral on Mount Saint Alban in Washington, D.C., followed by high tea in the tower. Treat it was indeed—I feasted my eyes on exquisite architecture with flying buttresses and fascinating downspouts, saw the sun shine through a glorious rose window, knelt in the Children's Chapel, dined on tasty pastries, enjoyed spectacular views of our nation's capital, and walked with my daughter through historical and holy spaces. Oh, yes, quite a treat.

When we entered the gift shop, I was drawn to a simple pencil sketch of the head of Jesus holding a little lamb in his arm in a way that showed the nail-pierced wrist. Over the years I have purchased many copies of this humble, comforting portrait of the Good Shepherd by Katherine Brown to give to people in hospice or crisis situations. It transforms a dull hospital bulletin board instantly and is an inviting addition to a children's worship center. I framed a copy, and it calms me every time I gaze upon it, especially in my darkest loneliest hours. The Good Shepherd calls me by name and lays down his life for his sheep. (See John 10:1-15.) The Good Shepherd will leave the ninety-nine and search for the lost one until he has found me. (See Luke 15:3-7.)

In the Twenty-third Psalm, often referred to as the Good Shepherd Psalm, we find more powerful words of comfort and security under God's watchful care. "Even though I walk through the darkest valley, I fear no evil; for you are with me" (v. 4). We find a lovely image of God as shepherd in Isaiah 40:11: "He will feed his flock like a shepherd; he will gather the lambs in his arms, and carry them in his bosom, and gently lead the mother sheep." We do not have to depend on our pea-size brains and skimpy little hearts. God's mercy will give us what we need each and every day no matter what. When we face difficult times, we can hold on to hope. Bereavement, financial struggles, health problems, whatever hurts our souls today will be okay in the end.

I make that last statement confidently because of powerful words found in scripture. Through the Bible, God whispers, "If you get lost, I will find you. You mean so much I will leave the ninety-nine. I know you; I call you by name. You are precious to me, and I love you." God's steadfast love and limitless care have propelled me along my journey in grief. I will always miss my beloved Irishman, but his love, God's love, and the love of family and friends have filled me to overflowing. Now I fondly hope to spill over this love into the world with powerful words of assurance, comfort, affirmation, and validation.

PRAYER: *Loving and generous God, flow through me so that the world may know your love and live boldly in your transforming power. Amen.*

THOUGHT FOR THE DAY: God's love for us invites us to love others more.

BROKEN OPEN

READ ISAIAH 49:13.

Sing for joy, O heavens, and exult, O earth;
break forth, O mountains, into singing!
For the LORD has comforted his people,
and will have compassion on his suffering ones.

ISAIAH 49:13

Twice a month my church serves the evening meal at a place called Urban Ministries in downtown Durham. Many churches and organizations come together to support this amazing place that provides housing, meals, counseling, several twelve-step programs, worship, a food pantry, and a clothing store. Church members inquired if the people wanted a different menu than usual, and the response was no. They like the lasagna with meat sauce, salad, large buttered roll, fruit cocktail, and large cookie. If anything, they would like more cookies.

The dining room doors open at 6:30 p.m. and close at 8:00 p.m. One Wednesday night the team scrambled to keep the line flowing. People kept coming—one after another, men, women, children—grateful to receive the free meal. The stream never let up, and we began taking extra rolls out of the pantry and scrounging for cupcakes and anything sweet to replace the cookies. We watched with concern as we got down to our last serving of lasagna. Like the miracle of the loaves and fishes, somehow everyone got fed. We wiped our brows, removed our latex gloves, and thanked the God who supplies our every need. It was then we learned that we had served 252 people—a new record.

On one of our less busy nights, I finished my chores and went out into the dining room to sit at one of the tables with a young mother and her toddler, a little boy with dark curly hair and big brown eyes. The child took one look at me and raised his arms for me to take him. He cuddled up close while I softly rocked back and forth. Such hospitality of spirits we had for each other.

I tried to engage his mother in conversation and quickly discerned she had a speech impediment. The two had been residents for three months while she was getting job training. But employment would be difficult with her speech problem. I wondered if she had a hearing deficiency as well. The child fussed when it came time to leave, and I handed him back to his mother. There is a German word *Christophel* that means "Christ-carrier." Love reached out—child to grandmotherly widow and grandmother to child. We gave and received of each other.

During the journey of bereavement, we sometimes turn inward, and life becomes all about us. In recent months it seems I have experienced a transformation where my broken heart broke open, and I was found by the God-connection that heals, comforts, and pushes us out of ourselves. The more I engage in loving acts of respect and dignity for myself and others, the more encounters I want. I feel I have reached a stage in my grief when I have started singing a song of joy. Just as the heavens, the earth, and the mountains sing and rejoice, I break into a song of gratitude and rejoicing for all that has been, is now, and will be. Thanks be to God!

PRAYER: *The cry of my heart is to know you, Lord, and to serve you by serving others. Thank you for your grace and love that brings me closer to you and my neighbors. Amen.*

THOUGHT FOR THE DAY: If we live for Christ, our hearts break open with gratitude and joy.

ON THE ROAD

READ LUKE 24: 13-35.

---

*[Two disciples] said to each other, "Were not our hearts
burning within us while [Jesus] was talking to us on the
road, while he was opening the scriptures to us?"*

LUKE 24:32

The two disciples returning to Emmaus are so absorbed in their disappointments and problems, their dashed hopes and frustrated plans, they don't recognize that the man who joins them and walks alongside them is Jesus. He asks what they are discussing. The disciples explain their sadness and confusion about the crucifixion and the empty tomb of their teacher, Jesus. The disciples are counting on him to rescue Israel from Roman occupation, and they believe the Old Testament prophecies point to a military and political messiah. When Jesus dies they lose all hope. They know the tomb is empty, but they do not understand that Jesus has risen; they cannot comprehend a living, breathing Jesus in their midst.

As Jesus and the disciples walk, Jesus responds to their despair by reintroducing the Old Testament prophecies and salvation history. Later at table with them, he takes bread, blesses it, breaks it, and gives it to them. Suddenly the blinders fall away, and the disciples recognize him. Jesus disappears, and then they ask each other, "Were not our hearts burning within us while he talked with us on the road and opened the Scriptures to us?" They rush seven miles back to Jerusalem to tell the others the good news that Jesus is alive. Alleluia! Emmanuel—God-with-us, Jesus-with-us—is risen! Alleluia!

Two years have passed since I began this phase of my life without my husband, my companion, my sweetheart. Along with the stretches of deep sadness and confusion, I saw clear transitions that gave me hope. A softening of my grief followed the first six months of heavy grief. After the first year of mourning, I wrestled with identity. I asked myself, *Who am I now that I am no longer wife and caregiver? Who I was before marriage? What dreams did I entertain for myself? Where has God offered me bliss in my life?* I have answered some of these questions, and others unfold and surprise me as I travel the road of grief.

Even after two years, the odyssey continues. I walk in the rain, walk in the dark, walk in the snow and ice, walk around in circles, walk backward. A practice of daily prayer, scripture reading, and meditation keep me going even when I have blisters on my feet and no longer want to walk. Day after day, month after month—even when in total confusion and various stages of mourning—I've been on the road. I may find myself a bit travel weary, but I know with absolute certainty I am never alone. My Lord, my steadfast travel companion, walks with me and talks about things that make my heart burn within me. I'm a deeper, more compassionate, humbler pilgrim for the experience. But there is more to learn about the Mysterious Other who showers us with grace and mercy and walks with us on the road—a journey that is blessed, surprising, and new every morning.

PRAYER: *Almighty God—Father, Son, and Holy Spirit—my heart overflows with gratitude for the journey and the conversation on the road with you. May I step into your presence daily and learn of your limitless love for me. May I then share the good news with other pilgrims on the journey. Amen.*

THOUGHT FOR THE DAY: God is with us on the road; we are never alone.

ABOUT THE AUTHOR

Nell Noonan is the author of *Not Alone: Encouragement for Caregivers* and *The Struggles of Caregiving: 28 Days of Prayer*. She served in church educational ministry for more than thirty years and also worked in public, school, and university libraries. Nell holds two master's degrees—one in religious education and one in library science. She also holds a Doctor of Ministry in biblical studies.

CPSIA information can be obtained at www.ICGtesting.com
Printed in the USA
LVOW10s1210120915

453712LV00001B/1/P